kate hughes

everygirl's
guide to
feminism

LONGMAN

An imprint of
son Wesley Longman

For Alex and Owen!

Addison Wesley Longman Australia Pty Limited
95 Coventry Street
South Melbourne 3205 Australia

Offices in Sydney, Brisbane and Perth, and associated companies throughout the world.

Cover and text designed by Lyndell Board
Edited by Margaret Trudgeon
Set in 10/12.5pt Esprit Book
Cover photograph courtesy of International Photographic Library
Printed in Malaysia

Hughes, Kate Pritchard, 1961–
    Everygirl's guide to feminism.

    Bibliography.
    ISBN 0 7339 0267 7

    1. Feminism. I. Title.

305.42

WITHDRAWN

contents

by Natasha Stott Despoja

'Everygirl's Guide to Feminism' is a great title because feminism is, and should be, for every girl. Regardless of your race, age, sexuality, wherever you live, whatever career you carve out, or hobbies you hold dear, however you like to dress, whether you are quiet or loud, want to have ten children or none—feminism has a lot to offer.

Feminism is about choices. There is no one feminism, it is a multi-headed beauty, a movement with a history as old as humanity. The more you understand about feminism, the more you will understand the world.

There was a time when it was generally believed:

- only white, land-owning men should vote;
- higher education would rot women's reproductive organs;
- ladies should never show their knees in public;
- sex is something wives just had to put up with in order to have children.

People may argue that things have changed, but the ripples of history are still felt today. Ask yourself how you and your family might be different if your great grandmother had been allowed to go to university and study medicine or law or any number of other professions from which women were excluded. How different would our society be if everybody's grandmother had been free to pursue the options men were allowed? We might have more women in Parliament now if they had.

Feminism has obviously brought a lot of changes in our world, but it is not just something that happens around you. An understanding of feminism may also change you. Symptoms, including more self-confidence, energy, and happiness, have been reported. Feminism can also equip you to change the world, and the first step is realising that change is possible. We can vote, go to university, enjoy our sexuality and show our knees in public now.

What do we want to achieve in the next 50 years? What do we want to achieve for our great grandchildren?

Don't just read this book—underline and scribble in the margins. You do not have to agree with everything. Developing your own ideas is part of what feminism is about. Write a letter about the issues to your grandmother or your grand daughter. Share the book with a friend or lend it to your brother and talk about it.

Change can be challenging and it is something we are going to have to do together. Maybe the next publication will be titled 'Every boys guide to feminism'.

Canberra
March 1998

acknowledgments

There are a number of people to gratefully thank for their help with this book. I've put them in alphabetical order! Firstly, Dr Sarah Buckley for discussing with me some of the material covered in this book and in particular for her help with alternative medicine. Katherine Henderson and Colin Thornton for lending me the house and computer in Darwin to write Chapter Four. Emrys Hughes for his sarcastic comments and assistance with media issues. Dr Nick Lennox for jokes about feminism and help with the medical stuff. Nici Lindsay, Elise Loukides and Jo Pollett for taking the time to read and comment on the drafts. Andrew Palmer for talking about the idea for the book in the first place and helping with legal matters. Claire Pollet-Sutton for her impressive expertise in matters to do with beauty. Nicola Thompson for making me cups of strong expresso coffee and reading and discussing it every inch of the way. Lynette Thorstensen for comments and encouragement and a good deal of support. Diane Walton for her photography. Finally, Peter Van Vliet, Emma Kelly and Margaret Trudgeon from Addison Wesley Longman. Peter because he was the publisher and was always so encouraging, professional and cheerful. Emma because, after much deliberation, she came up with such a good title. Margaret, for being the best editor. Many thanks to you all.

chapter

one

the 'F' word:
what is feminism?

It's called the 'F' word for two reasons. Firstly because it reminds people of another 'F' word and they seem to go together. Secondly, because people are afraid of saying 'feminism' out loud, as if it will instantly turn them into a social leper. This is particularly true for those who are inclined to go all the way and actually call themselves a feminist. It's almost enough to kill any conversation dead!

In this book I am going to try to account for these things. But before I do, you are going on a cook's tour of feminism to discover what it is and what it has achieved during the twentieth century (which is, however you look at it, an awesome amount!). By the end of this tour you will be able to understand what makes feminism and feminists tick.

If you were to take a snapshot of the lives of women at the start of the twentieth century and their lives at the end of the twentieth century, the differences would be unbelievable. Feminism began largely as a campaign to get one thing—the vote—because until the early part of the century women were not considered worthy of voting. Looking back, it seems difficult to understand the reasoning for this, but it was connected to the ways in which women were perceived. In a nutshell, they were perceived to be very much inferior to men, and incapable of making a rational decision—such as who to vote for.

Those who disagreed with this argued that women and men were not very different really, that they had the same levels of intelligence and rationality, and therefore should have the same rights of citizenship to vote and also to stand for parliament themselves. They brought this claim to everyone's attention using what we'd call today 'direct action'—they chained themselves to government buildings, they campaigned, they disrupted public events. Eventually they were successful and by the 1930s most women in the Western world had the vote. New Zealand was the first to enfranchise women in 1893, followed by Australia in 1902 (for federal elections), the United States in 1920, and finally the United Kingdom in 1928.

Women thought that with the vote won they would be able to change their world. They thought that it would lead to changes in the law, and to changes in social attitudes which would sweep in all sorts of improvements. However, they were wrong.

There was a bit of a lull in the feminist movement during the years between 1930 and 1960. When the Second World War started and the men went off to serve their country they left huge gaps in the workforce which women had to fill. The governments of the day spent a great deal of effort persuading women who had been housewives and mothers that they were capable of doing the kinds of manual labour that their husbands had done. This wasn't an easy task given that women had been conditioned to believe that their 'natural' place was in the home. But they managed to convince them and women started to do all kinds of work—in shipyards, in armaments factories, on the land, in hospitals at the front, as ambulance drivers, as bank tellers—in all sorts of occupations which had previously been regarded as 'men's work'.

The tricky bit came when a decision had to be made about what to pay the women for their work. Just because they were women they were paid less. How *much* less was worked out in various complicated ways. For the women themselves, while they suffered the loss of their fathers, brothers, husbands and sons (either temporarily or, for some, permanently), they soon discovered through force of circumstance that they could do the kinds of work which previously had been earmarked as far too difficult for them—just because they were women.

When the Second World War finished the men came home wanting their jobs back and a wife to look after them. And that is what they got! It wasn't all that easy to persuade women to leave the jobs they had been doing, because they had been earning more money than they had ever had before, and many had enjoyed the freedom and choice that this had brought with it. But the governments of the day campaigned hard to convince these women that their role was now to make the returning soldiers' lives as easy as possible. So it followed that the women left their jobs and went back into the home.

Once in the home they had no doubt what the job in hand was—to have babies! And this is what they did. They had lots. Their children are those we now call the 'baby boomers' because the birth rate went up amazingly during the years between 1945 and 1960. This was a time some politicians are still keen on today and try to recreate (probably because they feel nostalgic about their own childhood!). Our image of it now is one of picket fences, a home in the suburbs, a happily married couple with their three children and a dog, a man with a job and a woman who was a housewife. She was the one who cooked, cleaned, looked after everyone and was there when the children came home from school with the after-school snacks on tap. These are the images we see even today in advertisements because they seem to symbolise all that is good in the world. Everyone was happy!

But were they?

Into this idyllic picture crept something else. It began with a book from America in 1963 called *The Feminine Mystique* which was written by Betty Friedan, a not-so-happy housewife. In this book she talks about what life for such a housewife was like—a never-ending cycle of cleaning, feeding and caring. For everyone else in the family it was wonderful because there was always someone there to meet their needs. But the housewife had no one to meet her's. One of the catch cries of Friedan was 'Is this all?'.

But it wasn't just the emotional cost to women of caring for everyone else which was at issue. There were also other obstacles in society which meant they were treated so much worse than men. They didn't have equal pay for doing the same job as men. Many occupations had a rule that women who married had to leave. There was the 'sexual double standard', where men were allowed to be boys, but women who slept with more than one man were called 'tarts', 'whores' or 'slags'. It was legal for men to rape their wives. If someone else raped them they were likely to have their private lives taken apart in court in the attempt to paint them as a 'whore', so that the man on trial was seen as less guilty than he would have been if she was 'chaste'. If a couple divorced, and the woman had been a housewife, she would be left with almost nothing because she was not seen to have made a contribution to the marriage (this alone made divorce relatively unusual). Very few women went to university or qualified as professionals. If they worked, like today, it was most likely to be in low-paid, part-time work with no job security.

These are some of the issues which were reckoned up towards the end of the 1960s, and because of this the 1960s is the time when modern-day feminism is thought to have really begun. As you can see from the above short list of some of the ways in which women were discriminated against it was not a good look. Many women around the world began to think about this, and about some of the ways it might be possible to make things better. Others also tried to work out the causes of this situation. Was it because women and men were genetically different? Was there a genetic reason why it was OK for men to have numerous sexual relationships while it was taboo for women to do the same thing? Was it because we just raised children in such a way as to produce girls who were interested in the home and in having children, and boys who were interested in the workplace and in sport? Or were we born that way? Were men smarter than women? Were women closer to nature than men because they had babies? Was it all because of hormones? Did we live in a society which systematically discriminated against women because it was run by men who wanted to keep the best for themselves and the worst for women? These are just a few of the questions which people were grappling with as the 1960s moved into the 1970s.

Which brings us to feminism. Or, more accurately, to a variety of ideas about these questions and a variety of ways of dealing with how to improve things for women (and, some would argue, for men too) which have come to be grouped under the umbrella of 'feminism'.

Liberal feminism

Perhaps the most widely known kind of feminism, and the earliest to emerge, is known as liberal feminism. Liberal feminism argues that women and men are really very similar. They have the same capacities, the same level of intelligence, many of the same physical abilities and the same ability to think. These were the arguments used at the turn of the century to argue that women should be able to vote in elections.

Liberal feminists looked at the second class status of women and saw the cause of it in the way society was organised and run. They zeroed in on some of the most powerful institutions in society such as education, parliament, the legal system, the medical system and the workforce and saw that they all treated women and men differently. More to the point, they saw that women came off worst in them all. They didn't really have an answer for the question of *why* it was like this, apart from the fact that we raised girls and boys to have different abilities and interests so that they moved in different directions.

But they did have a solution, and it was a relatively easy one on paper. They believed in a two-pronged attack. Firstly, girls and boys should be brought up with equal opportunities. That is to say, girls should be encouraged to take maths and sciences, and should be encouraged to enjoy sport. Boys, on the other hand, should be taught to cook and look after babies and to enter professions such as nursing, childcare and teaching, so that the full range of occupations would be entered into by both men and women, which would lead to greater understanding between the two sexes and greater co-operation.

Secondly, they worked to create a more level playing field. This was to be done by trying to make sure that women occupied 50 per cent of all the powerful positions in society, so they would become 50 per cent of parliamentarians, 50 per cent of lawyers and judges, 50 per cent of professors in universities, 50 per cent of surgeons and so on. It was thought that if this could be achieved, then society would be changed for the better—not just for the women who worked at this level, but because their influence would change the nature of these institutions for the better.

And this is what they set about doing, some would argue very successfully. They managed to get changes made to the law so that, for example, women could receive 50 per cent of their marital property when they divorced; they won equal pay for women; they got equal opportunity legislation adopted so people could no longer legally discriminate against women in the workplace; they got a range of educational initiatives into the schools which encouraged girls to persevere with maths and sciences and so have access to more prestigious jobs; childcare places were multiplied and sexual harass-ment measures were put in place. All these things were aimed at creating this level playing field so that men and women could com-pete equally in the public world of work. If women did less well, it wasn't because they were discriminated against, but because they just weren't as good as the men.

In later years this has been challenged by those who believe that women just have more to deal with than men. One of these things is children. Because women are generally given the responsibility for children, whether they are in a relationship or not, this means they not only take time off work to look after then when they are born and when they are little, but it means they have to be available if the children are ill, have to arrange for them to be looked after when school finishes at 3 o'clock and in the holidays. All this means that women find it less easy to advance in their profession, have to take time off work and often end up taking part-time jobs which can accommodate these other demands. It can be argued that all this is just habit, that there is no reason why men couldn't do these things, or that they can be shared, but the overwhelming evidence shows that this just doesn't happen and the result is that women suffer.

Radical feminism

This leads me to another kind of feminism which might have some answers to these perplexing questions—radical feminism. This is the other really famous kind, most associated with bra-burning fanatics with short hair and arm pits which look like they have got someone in a permanent headlock. Not so!

Radical feminism takes as its starting point that there are fundamental differences between women and men. One of these (not surprisingly!) is their bodies. Having different bodies has meant, on the whole, that society has been organised traditionally so that men get access to the services of women. These services can be personal (all your clothes washed, your meals cooked and the kids well brought up), sexual (sex whenever you are in the mood), and emotional (someone to listen to you rave on about the football results, or anything else which is bothering you).

So, unlike liberal feminists who see discrimination against women as a sort of accident and sexism as a personal problem like BO, radical feminists think it is basic to the way our society functions. Another difference between them is that whilst liberal feminists concentrated on the 'public' sphere—the world of work, the law, government— radical feminists were more interested in 'personal' things—the sexual exploitation of women in pornography and advertising, the use of women's bodies in reproductive technology, domestic violence, the sexual abuse of women and children and so on.

Perhaps one of the reasons why radical feminism gets such bad press (literally!) is because it deals with things which make people uncomfortable. Perhaps one of the triumphs of liberal feminism is that you would rarely find someone these days who would seriously argue that women should be paid less than men, shouldn't vote, shouldn't be able to prosecute their husband for raping them. But when it comes to more personal—or sexual—things it gets more difficult.

There is little doubt that men are more violent than women, that women's bodies *are* used in an exploitative way in pornography to please men, that women are raped and abused, and that medical technology is not always used in a humane way on women. But this is something not many people want to see, or do anything about, because it disrupts the idea that men, on the whole, are nice to women. It also invites women and men to think about their own relationships or tastes and the power that is invested in them. And this makes them uncomfortable.

This might be a reason for the bad press, but it might also be because the presses are owned and run by men who are keen to keep things as they are, so portraying radical feminists who raise these issues as being completely deranged means that the woman in the street is much less likely to listen to what they have to say.

Like the liberal feminists, radical feminists have plans to change our communities. One of these, and perhaps the most effective, is to convince individual women that they don't have to put up with things and to provide them with practical services which help them to get out of bad situations—women's refuges and counselling for survivors of rape are examples of these. They also aim to raise public awareness of issues which impact badly on women and children. The increase of attention paid to child sexual assault and domestic violence, and the resulting government initiatives to deal with it, are both examples of this. Their pressure on 'beauty' pageants—where women walk around in bikinis after lots of cosmetic surgery, wearing heaps of make-up, being judged by old men—has practically put an end to them.

For some radical feminists, being involved with men is just too dangerous and unpleasant to contemplate. They also argue it is important not to sleep with the enemy, but with those who will look after you—with women. Most girls and women have a best friend who sees them through all manner of problems and who sticks by them through the thick and thin of men, children, divorce and death. In fact, such relationships are often more enduring than any other. So why are they placed second in a woman's life? Some radical feminists say they should be put first—emotionally, sexually and politically, because until women stop giving men all the services that they want, nothing will change.

Socialist feminism

The next major stream of feminism you need to know about is called socialist feminism. This kind uses some similar ideas to radical feminism—the most important one being that contemporary societies are largely 'patriarchal'. In other words, they are organised by men to serve the purposes of men, both as individuals and as a group. If you look at all the major power brokers in any society—universities, industry, the media, the police force, parliament, the public service, the medical system, the legal system and the military—you would be hard pressed to find any women at the top. They are almost all run by men! On an individual basis, men run families, earn income and hold power over women and children. Socialist feminists believe this to be the case.

But they add something else to the equation, and that is the economy. In a capitalist society like ours where (male) individuals own all the large corporations and businesses rather than the community collectively owning them, it is likely that these owners will organise things so that profits go up and men will benefit from this. What this means in practice is that women, for various reasons, never earn what men do and that work is organised in terms of hours, childcare provision and the qualities you need to get to the top (such as competitiveness and aggression rather than co-operation) giving men a distinct advantage over women.

They also link some of the 'personal' issues dealt with by radical feminism (such as pornography and sex work) to profit, and argue that in a society designed to please men, where men have money to consume things, they will want to consume women in various ways.

It might sound from this that there is a conspiracy going on! That there is a group of powerful men who secretly meet and plot and plan together to ensure women get a bad deal! Well, this is a little unlikely.

Instead, our society is the result of a long history of male domination and although it is constant, it changes. One example of this (which Naomi Wolf wrote about in her book *The Beauty Myth*) is that as women have gained a little bit more power in the workforce, a new pressure has emerged—the pressure to look 'good'. She argues that the cosmetic industry, the dieting industry, the clothing industry and cosmetic surgery have all cranked up their operations in the last ten years. Now women have been persuaded that unless they look like a surgically enhanced stick insect wearing Versace clothing they can never be happy or successful in the workplace. In fact, it looks like the last bit might be true! But these industries are ultimately about profit and their effect is upon women —and it is not a good one because women are under increasing pressure to conform to a 'beauty' standard set by the men who run the companies. We'll look at some of these issues later on.

Just before we finish this tour, there is one more type of feminism to mention briefly (you were warned!).

So you're hanging out in the ocean & the first wave of feminism has gone & the second wave & who knows how many other waves. It's dead flat & you find yourself thinking, Feminism - who needs it?

Aren't we post-feminist now?

Just be sure you can tell a fin de siecle from a fin de shark

horacek

Eco-feminism

Eco-feminism is a relatively new form which has arisen since we became aware that we are wreaking environmental destruction. We know it is happening, but some have tried to answer the more important question of why. The answer is linked, not surprisingly, to capitalism and to patriarchy. We see the earth as something to be exploited—we dig out minerals, we remove oil, we use ridiculous amounts of chemical fertilisers to make the soil produce more and more, we use nuclear fuel and so on. All these resources will end one day and their use and abuse means we have changed the earth's balance irrevocably. It also means our health is affected.

So why? Eco-feminists think it is because of men's mindset which is an exploitative mindset. Just in the same way that women are used up, mother nature is used up. There are better ways of doing things; using solar power, using organic fertilisers, leaving uranium in the ground rather than using it to make nuclear bombs. But these don't make profits to the same extent. Eco-feminists believe that if we are sensible, and especially if we want future generations to have any kind of life, it is the patriarchal mindset we need to change because it is the cause of our environmental nightmare.

But wait, there's more! Psychoanalytic feminism (it's all in our heads), Marxist feminism (it's capitalism's fault), French feminism (women have a better way of thinking and writing), Poststructuralist feminism (we are constantly changing and defining ourselves through the ideas in society which are available), Postmodern feminism (maybe there are no such things as oppressors and victims—just individuals), Cultural feminism (women have special qualities which we need to value and use and not put down) . . . But I'll leave these to you.

As a group then, feminists believe in one thing—that our society is run by men largely for their own benefit and that to change this would bring enormous benefits to women and some would say to men too. Part of living in a patriarchy, for men, means a system of domination too. Not all men rejoice at the idea of women being done over, and many actively try to stop it. Not all men think that patriarchy is a brilliant system, because they see the casualties of it in the lives of their daughters, sisters, mothers and wives. Even for themselves, some men object to being dominated by older men, heterosexual men, richer men, and believe there is a better way to go which involves some of the feminist ideas we have looked at here.

In the next chapter we will move away from theory and look at feminists themselves—at what they do, how they look and what they believe in.

chapter

chapter
two

humourless feminists:
the myths

There are a lot of myths about feminists. In this chapter I am going to start by going through a few of these and offer you a more realistic picture of what make feminists tick.

Myth no. 1: They have no sense of humour

OK, so why is it that feminists are thought to have no sense of humour? In my experience this is very far from the truth! But ideas about power and so on often circulate through jokes. Everyone must have been in the situation where someone is telling a revolting joke about a racial group of some kind and maybe laughed and maybe thought 'Mmn, is it that funny?'. The same goes for jokes about women which put them down, which aim at their bodies or their intelligence.

If you point this out, the joker always says 'But it's only a JOKE' which means 'listen to the message'. It is almost as if the joke bit is a cloak which covers a message—whether it be one which has a go at women or at a racial or ethnic group, the joker really wants to insult. And because it is a 'joke' you come across as having no sense of humour if you are not joining in. I guess such a message is not one best passed on or laughed about. Particularly because there are always better ones to tell.

Myth no. 2: They are aggressive

The second myth about feminists which does the rounds is that they are aggressive. Of course, unlike men, it is thought most unattractive for women to be aggressive. The first thing to say about this is that, incredibly, the achievements feminists have made through this century have been made without any aggression. This is quite unusual if you think about it. Most social movements which have the aim of changing society in some way have engaged with aggression—even violence—at some point. Often this is not sought by them, but happens.

As a movement then, the women's movement has been remarkably calm. It has achieved its ends through peaceful means. Why this is so, is not clear. We know that women as a group tend to shy away from violence and are more likely to be victims of it than perpetrators of it. Even when women are subjected to the kinds of stress which would make some men start to shout and reach for the nearest blunt instrument, women tend not to do this. As a rule, they don't even get violent through alcohol, which people often think is the trigger for men. Instead, some argue that they internalise the stress and it emerges through depression, or eating disorders or some such thing. This might be simply because of the way women are brought up—to be passive. Small boys, on the other hand, are much more likely to feel comfortable with fighting physically and with protecting themselves. For girls, this is not 'ladylike'.

So this myth that feminists are aggressive doesn't seem to be borne out if you look at the history of the women's movement, nor if you look at the way modern women negotiate stress or conflict. But this doesn't mean that feminists are as passive as they are meant to be. It seems to be that they are what you might call assertive, which is different. Being assertive means standing your ground and resisting things which are not good for you. It means not being bullied, and stating your case.

A friend told me a story recently which illustrates this point. She came home with her

partner and another male friend to find their neighbour from over the road at fever pitch because their friend had parked his car, by mistake, in a spot the neighbour liked. The neighbour (you see I didn't even have to tell you it was a man did I?!) was shouting and swearing and trying to swing a punch at the other men. And they say women are 'emotional'!

My friend (who calls herself a feminist) intervened because she thought they might start to physically fight. She was assertive, which means she said the parking spot wasn't *his*, but that if he cared so much about it they could just move the car. Which they did. The neighbour calmed down but called her an 'aggressive bitch'. Maybe the label is used just to insult women and to suggest that not being frightened and passive means they are 'unfeminine' in some way. In fact, they are refusing to be bullied and that is all.

Myth no. 3: They want to take over the world

The next myth to examine is one I have heard a million times. Feminists want to take over the world. This is usually elaborated upon by envisioning a world where women run the army, the police force, the government, the universities, industry, the legal system and so on, and do it in a ridiculous way. You know, there is 'menstruation leave' in the workplace, the government can never make its mind up about anything, the law always gives females the benefit of the doubt, the army is too busy putting on nail varnish and hair spray to get organised etc. etc. Oh, and I forgot, men are discriminated against everywhere and only kept for sex. Does this sound familiar?!

It could be on one level that those who imagine such things are afraid of being in the position that women are in contemporary society. In other words, that they see a realistic picture of patriarchy, and the thought of being in a subordinate position fills them with fear. It also fuels all those prejudices about women—that they are unintelligent, disorganised, easily influenced, vain and silly.

But do feminists want to take over the world? There are two answers to this. Firstly, the liberal feminists who I discussed in the last chapter are certainly interested in trying to get women into positions of power so that they might be better at protecting the interests of women. If, for example, half the judges in the courts were women, would they be more sympathetic towards women than men are? If 50 per cent of our politicians were women, would that mean a different culture in the parliament, a hope of better community services? More resources given to hospitals and schools? So far we have had no chance to find this out. But it might be because of the way powerful institutions are run, and the values they are based on. They are run hierarchically and favour qualities such as competition and individualism and do not value (for the most part) empathy or co-operation. These are qualities which suit men better than they suit women. It may be that it doesn't matter whether you are male or female because if you have these qualities and are working in these institutions you are part of that organisation and part of those values. In other words, if you display what are thought to be 'female' or 'feminine' characteristics such as nurturance, conciliation and empathy, you will not get very far!

The second part of the answer to the question 'Do feminists want to take over the world?' might be a 'yes', but it is quickly followed by 'but they would rather change the world'. The qualities which are associated with femininity mentioned above are thought, in our society, to be rather silly. Weak. Inefficient. Not cost effective. Woosy. And so on.

But some feminists argue that it would be a much better society if they were respected. Imagine, for example, a government whose aim was to make sure that everyone was well educated and whose health system was second to none. Where community services existed which ensured that old people, people with disabilities and children were nurtured and cared for. Where the feminine charac-teristics, rather than masculine ones, were the basis upon which all the institutions were run and were thought to be the pinnacle of human morality and integrity. It would mean a world where boys were taught not to be violent, just as girls are today, and to be strong, nurturing and caring, rather than individualistic and competitive. Even the parliament itself would have to change from a system where the government and the opposition clash and try to thrash the others in arguments, to beat them in fact.

It sounds like a science fiction novel doesn't it?

But many feminists argue that the transformation of what we have now to something like this is what we ought to be aiming for because it would mean a richer, more humane and an ultimately better society for everyone—men, women and children. But this is a difficult task because these values are seen as so weak and pathetic and anyone who displays them in these powerful institutions—especially a man—is thought to be in need of some counselling. It's thought to be more normal for women, but since there are so few around and they are forced to be tough to get on, the effect is negligible.

So, feminists do want a bigger say in how things are organised and some also would like to see a revamp of the qualities we value as a society, so that those seen as characteristic of women creep into the way we do things, and it would all be a good deal better.

Myth No. 4: All feminists are ugly'

OK, now for the classic one. Well, I can't say that in my experience there are hoards of ugly people flocking to sign up. Feminists are no uglier than anyone else!

But let us look at this word 'ugly' for a moment. In contemporary societies we have a much more rigid view of what 'beauty' and 'ugly' means for women than ever before. And we can be sure that these terms are pretty much always directed at women rather than men. 'Beauty' as a term seems to have not so much to do with the shape of a face or a body, but most often to do with what is done with the face or the body.

In other words, if you plaster yourself with moisturiser, foundation, blusher, mascara, eye shadow, perfume and lipstick (there might be more, I just can't think of them all), exfoliate, use electrolysis, have cosmetic surgery, dye your hair, cut your hair, curl your hair, diet, wear revealing clothes and high heels—you might be lucky enough to get called 'good-looking'. If you religiously read *Cleo* and go for all the products they advertise you might be off to a good start!

But it can go to ridiculous lengths. The other night I couldn't believe my eyes when I was watching an 'infotainment' show where they were discussing 'hand lifts'. In other words, you can go to a cosmetic surgeon who will do things to your hands to make them look younger! I forget what these things were but the hands looked exactly the same to me afterwards as they did at the start. Weirder still were the people saying it was worth every (pretty) penny and it had changed their lives and made them feel much better. The mind boggles!

Anyway, back to the 'feminists are ugly' joke. The point is that if you choose not to go in for all this stuff—the hair, the make-up, the clothes, the dieting and the cosmetic surgery, there is a good chance that you might be called 'ugly'. Oh dear! What a nightmare.

Later on, we will be looking at some of these issues in a bit more detail. For now, it is enough to say that what the label 'ugly' hinges on is whether heterosexual men find you appealing. Rumour has it that the more of the hair, the make-up, the clothes, the dieting and the cosmetic surgery you pay for, the more appealing you will be. Because these things are not just about the way you look, but also about the way you are supposed to act (nice and quietly), leaving them well alone means you might be open to allegations of 'ugliness' and 'not being attractive to men'.

Myth No. 5: Feminists are obsessed by gender

One of the things which all feminists share is a belief that men and women have very different kinds of lives. Furthermore, that men have much more than women in terms of money, life chances, value given to their ways of seeing things, respect given to them as people, freedom from being judged on what they look like and so on.

I called this a 'belief', but it is more than that because if you have even the most cursory glance at any research which measures well-being of groups in the community (things such as income, professional status, educational levels) it is obvious that there are real differences between the two sexes. These things are easy to quantify, to measure, but there are other things which are less easy—self-esteem, feelings of wellbeing, self-respect, confidence—which you can't really measure using numbers. Some would argue that if you live in a society which values one sex above another and promotes its interests above another, then it is likely that these feelings will dominate the subordinated sex.

Sometimes it can come down to the simplest things. Reading the newspaper can be a case in point. OK, now I am going to admit that I am obsessed by gender, but in the newspaper I was reading yesterday, I noticed the following things. Firstly, they had a selection of notable quotes of the week. All nine were from men. Secondly, all the books reviewed were written by men. Thirdly, there were hardly any photos of women, but many of men. One of the photos which featured a woman and a man was accompanied by the headline 'John X and his wife leave the coroners court'. John X's 'wife' was, in fact, the *mother* of the person who had died, and John X was his stepfather. So what is her name? Why is she just an anonymous 'wife'? She was the dead man's *mother* for heaven's sake! Fourthly, an interview with a female politician was about being female. Full stop. Nothing about what she did in her job. Some of the questions included: How did she manage her domestic role? Did her children and husband mind her travelling? How does she cope with being a woman in parliament? How does she keep fit and slim? Can you imagine an interview with a male politician which concentrated on this funny business of him being a man? How does he manage to get his shirts ironed? Does he do them himself? How does he keep so slim and sexy? The point I want to make here is that the female politician is being problematised— made a problem—because she is a woman. The norm is being a man. It seems to me that asking her about her private life lacks, shall we say, respect?

If you wanted to, you could ignore these things in the newspaper, or ignore the differences in the way women and men are treated, but you can't say they are not there. Or, you could say that they don't matter. But I think they do matter because they do women a disservice. They also help to create a situation in which women, and women's lives, are marginalised and seen as secondary to the main game which is the game of men.

Having said that, and knowing that, it doesn't mean you have to be obsessed. You can watch action movies where men run around with guns killing people and laugh at the macho posturing as well as enjoying it. You can watch TV shows where the women act as if they need an emergency brain transplant. Of course, these women know not to come across like a genius if they want to keep their job just as they know how to look 'good'. It is about the culture we live in and the roles women are given within it.

Myth No. 6: We live in a post-feminist age now

Very annoying. Also tragically ill-informed. I prefer the t-shirt which reads 'I'll be a post-feminist in a post-patriarchy'.

People who repeat this myth usually quickly follow it with things like 'They have achieved everything. In fact, it is men who now need liberating'. You know, stuff like that. In fact, I read this just the other day in a (surprise surprise) newspaper. Oh dear me!

It is true that the second wave of feminism got cracking in the 1970s. It is true that they accomplished great things in the 1980s. And it is true that going into the twenty-first century feminism is more than alive and kicking. Why? Because we need it.

Usually the paid-up fans of this myth like to portray feminists as hopelessly out-of-date women in their forties and fifties who are just angry and bitter for personal reasons and have not moved with the times. This is just a variation of the 'hysterical woman' stereotype.

Well, I have got news for them. Currently, young women in their late teens and twenties are creating an adventurous and exciting new wave of feminism. Some of them, like Naomi Wolf, Rene Denfeld and Katie Roiphe (who are all American) have some criticisms of older styles of feminism because they think they portray women as victims. Obviously, these young women don't see themselves or any other woman as a victim of anything, but as people who are in charge of their lives, who can do what they like. This is always true up to a point, but as women get older their politics tend to get more radical (the opposite is true of men, interestingly enough) and they often get more feminist because they have had the life experience which tells them things are not as they seem when you are young.

But these are the young women who are writing the books. They are interesting to read because they have started to redefine what feminism means now and to look for new ways of dealing with the problems women face. But how many people read books about feminism? Apart from you?!

Aside from writers, there are millions of young women who are using all sorts of media to get their message across—the internet, `zines, magazines, music, film, cartoons. Maybe it is a sign of the times that these are the places we should look to get a handle on what is happening.

There are Riot grrrls (music), Grot grrrls (art), Revolution nrrrds (magazines), Game girls (computer game designers), Geekgirls (internet raiders)—even Spicegirls! They are all feminists, all interested in the ways these media can be used to promote the interests of women and help redefine the ways women are seen. But the point about them is that they don't wait around to be defined—but define themselves. They are very active.

One of the interesting strengths they all have is that they play around with image. In myth no. 4 ('All feminists are ugly') we looked at some of the ideological reasons for this myth. One of these is that if women are not presenting themselves with the express aim of pleasing men, they are seen as 'ugly'—a fate worse than death. But what these young women want to do is weaken the link between how you look, and what you are like. In other words, image can just be something you use for fun. One day you might dress as a corporate raider, another as a gothic vamp, another as a sex goddess. Or, then again, you might choose to wear low-cut dresses and heaps of make-up all the time.

The point is that you do it for yourself and not for anyone else. Furthermore, what you wear isn't the whole story. You might be seen in clothing which might be called 'sexually provocative' by some, but this doesn't mean you want to be, or even are. Long gone are the days when women's clothing is seen as responsible for men's actions, after all. What they wear is not, in the end, a predictor of what they are like at all.

These ways of thinking are reflected in the music, the internet `zines, the cartoons, the computer games where women who might (or might not) enjoy styles of femininity are shouting loudly and intelligently about the way they see the world and the things that they want from it. Foremost among these, not surprisingly, is to be treated as the smart and resourceful young women that they are.

Less certain, though, is the response to this from men. It's a really attractive idea to be so self-defined that it doesn't matter what people think about you. But when the dress codes in the society you live in have such rigid things to say about women, it's difficult to imagine that they are immune to these standards or that they won't be treated accordingly. But that is their risk and that is their choice.

So there you have it. Nearly everything you read about feminism in the popular media is silly. Feminists come in many forms, they are no more ugly or aggressive than anyone else. They tell jokes. They watch rubbish on TV. They want to change the world. And they are ALIVE.

chapter
three

fat is a feminist
issue: bodies

When surveys are done about what women would most like to achieve in their lives, forget careers, forget money, forget babies, forget happiness—it looks like most women would like to lose weight! Usually about seven kilos. In this chapter we are going to explore this bizarre phenomenon which has arisen at the end of the twentieth century, and try to explain the reasons for it.

In the last chapter we briefly discussed images of 'ugliness' and 'beauty' and the ways in which women might get assigned one of these two labels. For there is no doubt that this labelling is a major concern of women today. So why?

Naomi Wolf in her book *The Beauty Myth* suggests a number of reasons for it. She thinks that because women have achieved so much this century, such as equal pay, maternity leave, equal opportunity legislation, better laws and more sexual freedom, something else has been brought into play to counter this—the beauty myth. In other words, a number of large corporations and industries have effectively combined to place new pressures on women which will limit the way they can compete with men—especially in the workforce. Among these corporations and industries she counts the cosmetic industry, the diet industry, the fashion industry, the cosmetic surgery industry and the pornography industry.

She thinks that they have helped to create a culture—alongside the media, of course—where women are judged much more by how they look than anything else. These industries are growing at an enormous rate. In addition, more and more occupations (especially ones which women are involved in) have what she calls a PBQ (Professional Beauty Qualification). This means that in order to work within them, women have to conform to a very specific 'look'. No prizes for guessing what that 'look' is like! In the past, only people like flight attendants or newsreaders had to be young, slim and well turned-out. Flight attendants used to get weighed to make sure they were within the official limits!

But today, these demands are affecting more and more jobs. If you don't have this 'look', you can be seen as not fitting the image of the workplace. Because of this, women are having to spend more and more time and money on their appearance—on gyms, dieting, make-up, clothes and so on. Also, they are likely to be seen as past their 'use-by' date much earlier than men. Newsreaders are a good example of this. Know any female newsreaders over forty? Know any male newsreaders *under* forty? For men, age is thought to bring stature and wisdom, for women it is thought to bring ugliness.

Wolf doesn't suggest that these industries are in league with one another in any organised way, but the effect is the same, men and women workers are treated very differently. Not a good look.

Images of beauty

Some writers think that in Western cultures, women's bodies are seen like blank pages. What you write on them with clothes, make-up, hairstyles and shoes, signals to the world how available you are. I suppose an example of this would be the nun's habit as compared to a sex worker's clothes—the nun is not sexually available and the sex worker is. I am not suggesting that this is the truth, but it is how our society views women and their appearance.

What seems to be happening, then, is that there is increasing pressure on women to look 'beautiful', that is, to look available and to look attractive to men. When this is linked, as Wolf suggests, to your income as well, the pressure gets worse. So what does being 'beautiful' mean? It means being young (not possible for very long), slim (also known as hungry all the time and eventually depressed), probably being blond (dyed if necessary), having a mild tan (sun bed?), having large breasts (surgically enhanced if necessary), exercising so you have 'muscle definition' (exhausting), wearing make-up (expensive and messy) and wearing clothes which accentuate all of the above. The other thing about this image is that it is, on the whole, about white women, so if you're not white, that puts you out of the running straight away. Not fair! Or maybe it is a relief?

The media

Where does this image come from? Notice that I said 'image' rather than putting it in the plural, because it is pretty one-dimensional. Sometimes when I read trashy magazines featuring stories about famous actresses or TV stars, I find it really difficult to tell them apart. The reason for this is simple—they all share the same physical features, either by accident or design. Is there a factory somewhere?

But this takes us to what is usually seen as the source of the problem—the media. I mean by the media TV, film (both 'Hollywood' movies and pornographic films), advertising, music and magazines. Plus the fashion industry, of course. They all feed into one another in various ways. Actors become singers. Singers become actors. Models become actors. Soap opera stars become Hollywood film stars. They all advertise beauty products. They all of them appear in women's magazines and they are look pretty much the same (see above!).

Interestingly, although these women are perceived as the ideal woman in Western societies, much of their money-making activities are aimed at women rather than at men (apart from pornography). It is women, on the whole, who watch soap operas, respond to advertisements for beauty products, are interested in the new season's fashions and what gossip women's magazines have to tell about these women's private lives. What they are used for is to say to women 'if you buy this product you will look like me'. And linked to this, although less directly, is the notion that if you look like that you will have a fabulously happy life. All I can say about this is, what absolute rubbish!

Weight

All the women who appear in the media in various ways are thin. Make no mistake about it, this is unnatural. They are thin because they work very hard at it. I read in a women's magazine, for example, that Demi Moore who graced the cover of *Vanity Fair* in the last week or so of pregnancy and again a couple of weeks after giving birth looking 'perfect' exercised five hours a day to do this. I mean, in the gym.

They work out. They diet. They smoke. They have liposuction. Again, not a good look.

When there is such a dire lack of normal-looking women as role models in the media, it is not surprising that women want to look like the ones that are there. What choice is there? And add to that all the material around in magazines, 'infotainment' shows and advertisements which offer a non-stop diet (sorry!) of encouragement to look like that yourself—it makes it very difficult to escape.

Diets don't work. No matter how much you spend on them, or what you do or for how long, there is over a 90 per cent chance that within a year, your body will have returned to the shape it likes. The shape that is right for you. Obviously, if you take drastic measures like giving up food altogether or exercising to within an inch of your life, you may manage to maintain another shape.

Which brings us to the issue of eating disorders. Do you know how prevalent they are? Or how dangerous? They affect, in one form or another, about one in three women and girls. Girls of ten are now dieting. About 40 per cent of the female population are dieting at any

one moment in time. In *The Beauty Myth,* Naomi Wolf states that more women die of anorexia nervosa per year in the USA than people have died of AIDS since its beginnings. It's almost an epidemic.

Eating disorders come in a number of forms. At one extreme there is anorexia nervosa where women literally starve themselves—sometimes to death—because they believe they are too fat. Even when they look in the mirror they think this. Then there is bulimia nervosa where eating becomes out-of-control and the woman binges, then vomits. Here, almost normal weight can be maintained. At, perhaps, the least serious end of the spectrum, there is the constant dieting which the majority of women go in for. Even this has serious effects on health because metabolisms slow down (go into starvation mode), so any available food is turned into fat to help you to survive. Apparently, this way of living and eating most often causes women to become depressed—because they have to constantly deprive themselves of what their body needs and that is no fun at all.

Sometimes you have to wonder why there is nothing done about all this. It doesn't take a genius to figure out that eating disorders are linked somehow to our images of 'beauty' and the desire produced in women to look like that. So when people are dying and suffering as they are, why are these images allowed to be circulated? Surely there are better, healthier images than this.

Cosmetic surgery

When I teach classes of first year students—girls of eighteen and nineteen—and cosmetic surgery comes up, there are always at least two girls in the class (of eighteen or so) who admit they have had some. Astonishing. And the cosmetic surgery industry is growing at an incredible rate—much faster than any other kind of medicine. If you can call it medicine—a word usually reserved for procedures for making sick people healthy. Cosmetic surgery often makes healthy people sick.

Cosmetic surgery means having operations done which change the way you look. You can have nose jobs, breasts made bigger or smaller, face lifts, hand lifts, liposuction—which means having fat sucked out of you by a machine which looks like a vacuum cleaner—eyes made bigger or smaller, 'tummy tucks', lower ribs removed to make your waist smaller and so on and so on and so on. New 'procedures' are evolving on an almost daily basis. The point of all this is, once again, for women to conform to a cooked up version of what is 'beautiful' (to men).

Imagine you are a space traveller and you visit a planet where half the population has gone under the knife, or tried to drastically change the way they look, for the pleasure of the other half of the population. They stop eating, they dye their hair, they do exercises, change their eye colour with contact lenses, change the colour of their skin, they have unnecessary and dangerous operations. Wouldn't you think there was something seriously wrong there? I would. But that is what is happening right here, right now.

Why is it so important to women to be attractive to men? The obvious answer is so they can have relationships with them, I suppose. But it matters to women who are in relationships already—they don't stop caring. I think the real reason is because the way a woman looks, how far she goes to conform to the ideal, is a measure of her worth in our society. When women talk about body image, they mostly say that they do it all *for themselves*. In other words, they are not focussed completely on their attractiveness to men, but on their own feelings of self-worth. And, obviously, the more they feel they look like the Elle McPhersons, Cindy Crawfords and Danii Minogues (post-surgery!) of this world, the better they feel. Oh dear.

So what do men think about this? Are they obsessed about what women look like? Do they want to have relationships only with women who fit the bill? Everyone knows that the Rod Stewarts of this world—men in their fifties who insist on having relationships with women in their twenties with blond hair and everything else—might think looks are important. This is because, just as women might value themselves by their looks, some men think their importance is measured by their ability to parade around with 'good looking' women on their arms. But what about your average bloke? Research shows that most men say it doesn't matter half as much as other things such as a sense of humour, kindness and fidelity. Indeed, in a lot of surveys done, both sexes seem to overestimate how important looks are to the other sex. Women think men want women who are thin and everything else. Men think women want men who are fit and muscular. That they don't is a relief. But unlike men, women have enormous pressure on them to conform to this ideal.

Reproduction

So far we have been looking at women's bodies as objects—things to be looked at, and what that means for women. But women's bodies are also active things which can do a lot. Women's bodies are always in a state of change. Even naturally, they grow and shrink in different places at different times.

When you talk with people about the position of women in society, almost always the issue of babies come up as an explanation for why it is that women get a bad lot. So this is what we will look at now. This century, there has been a slow but strong decrease in the number of babies that women have. At the turn of the century, it was in the region of six per woman, and at the century's end, it is 1.8. That is a big difference. Furthermore, it is estimated that about 25 per cent of young women in their early twenties today will have no children at all. Some of these will want them but be unable to have them, but the vast majority will simply choose not to.

Such choice is possible, of course, because we have two things— contraception and abortion. Until the contraceptive pill was put on the market in 1961 the only available contraceptives were condoms, the diaphragm and the IUD (it hasn't changed much has it?). But the pill marked the beginning of the declining birth rate. Abortions were another solution to unwanted pregnancies, but until relatively recently they were illegal. They were carried out in people's houses who were liable to prosecution for performing them. It was very dangerous for their patients also, who were vulnerable to infection and a variety of problems which resulted from the procedure, and it was not unusual for them to die. Abortions are not new, they have been carried out for centuries in a variety of ways—some surgical and some using abortifacients (drugs). In the last century, potions for 'obstructed menses' (i.e. pregnancy!) were sold by chemists and advertised in magazines quite freely. But that was before they were made illegal.

So why were they made illegal in the first place? Many writers think it was because the government of the day wanted women to have babies, because having babies meant women stayed at home, out of the workforce and dependent on men. Even today, when the issue of abortion is raised (the moral issues aside) there is often an undercurrent of this way of thinking. In other words, women having babies and being at home, and men providing for them in a nuclear family, is somehow regarded as a 'natural' way of organising things. How wrong they are. There is nothing 'natural' about this at all, or everyone would be doing it unquestionably. But we are not. In fact, fewer and fewer people are doing it.

So why is this? Perhaps the most obvious reason why young women don't want to have babies is because they know it means their careers will suffer. And it might also mean they are dependent on men. Because divorce rates, and family breakdown rates, are so high, it is not unlikely that these young women will end up parenting on their own. About 85 per cent of single parent families are headed by women. So if all goes well and the marriage survives, the woman might have a lifetime of economic dependence on men because they are seen as primarily responsible for the care of the children and do their paid work around that. If it doesn't go well— as it doesn't in one out of three relationships—the likelihood is that she will effectively be a single parent, one of the poorest sections of the community.

Having said that, it seems unlikely to me that young women are making baby decisions on that basis, and more likely that they just simply don't want them, and prefer a life with more money and more freedom and more choice. Often the 'family values' brigade blame feminism for this—and they might be right because it is because of feminism, and women's new ability through education and expanding work opportunities to earn their own incomes, that the choice to be childless is a viable one.

Another possible reason for young women's reluctance to have babies is, again, to do with issues of 'beauty'. Having babies changes your body (surprise surprise!). Obviously, your uterus gets huge, your breasts get huge, there are stretch marks, there are varicose veins, you get hairier (something to do with hormones), and you put on weight. You put on weight because your body lays down supplies of fat to help you breastfeed which uses up a huge number of calories. Now, you probably shuddered as you read this because there is no doubt that the above list of changes to your body are not ones which are seen as part of beauty. And if I am right that young women (in fact, women generally) are deeply concerned with the way they look, they might well not put themselves through it! Some of these changes are temporary and some permanent (particularly the weight one).

So we have a problem here. We have a conflict. We have an idealised image of female beauty upon which women hang their self-esteem and it is an image which is not at all compatible with the short and long-term effects of childbearing. This reminds me of watching a horrendous documentary on TV about childbirth in which women talked about the choices they made about how to give birth. Among them was a model who chose to have a caesarean section rather than give birth naturally. Her reason? Because she thought her partner would no longer be able to see her as a sexual being if he saw her give birth. 'Yes,' her partner mournfully intoned, 'She is right'. How weird is *that*?! But it does point to a major conflict in contemporary society where maternity and sexuality are seen as mutually exclusive.

There is some evidence, however, that this is changing. It looks like pregnant women can now be recast as 'sexy' or, at least, 'beautiful'. In Australia recently there was a huge fuss about a pregnant woman who worked on a game show. She worked right up until the birth and soon after it returned to the show. But that wasn't the issue which caused the furore. What people objected to was she continued to wear revealing (also known as 'sexy') clothes which showed her expanding cleavage and her pregnant belly. She didn't hide a thing! And this is what the viewers objected to, judging by listening to talk-back radio and reading letters to the papers. There were others (mainly women) who thought it was marvellous, but people found it very confronting.

There are advertisements, also, which use pregnant women as symbols. Most often they are used as symbols of security (for example a car advertisement which said being in the car felt a bit like being in a womb), but sometimes also as people in need of security (most often in bank advertisements). Then there are the members of the beauty club like Demi Moore, Madonna and Elle Macpherson who have continued to display themselves as sexual beings as well as pregnant beings.

It might well be that with a few more years of this, young women might feel more at home with the idea of being pregnant and looking sexy. Maybe that is not a bad thing. But it would be so much better if women cared less about how they looked altogether and they valued themselves as the fantastic people they are, rather than by the size of their thighs. For, in the end, it doesn't really matter. It would be much better to see the female body—pregnant or not—as something you live in and use and enjoy rather than something to be looked at. Don't worry what people think of you, look the way you want to. And always remember—eat, drink and be merry.

chapter
four

the personal is political:
relationships

Relationships can be one of the most fraught areas of a person's life. But they can also determine how happy you are. Having rewarding, loving, respectful relationships is probably the key to a happy life in the end. Just as having relationships in which you are not respected or looked after or supported—or having few relationships at all—can lead to a life of loneliness and, ultimately, unhappiness. Some psychologists believe that being deprived of love, especially if you are a child, can be as detrimental to your health and wellbeing as being deprived of food or water.

Having said that, it is important to recognise that all relationships have elements of politics and power within them. In other words, there are outside influences in society which can affect very strongly the kind of relationship you will have with someone—despite your best intentions. We all live within societal structures which are informal (not written down), but which nevertheless have a very profound influence on you, and on your relationships. For example, in contemporary societies men have more power than women. They have more power in the 'public' world of the workplace, in politics, in the media, in religion, in the union movement and so on. They are automatically given more respect than women and are listened to seriously. So does this power influence their personal relationships with women in the 'private' sphere? I think the answer is 'yes'.

In the early days of second wave feminism it was thought that one of the ways to redress the imbalance between the sexes was to work from the grassroots. So as well as trying to change the institutions in the 'public' sphere such as those mentioned above so that they were more user-friendly for women and girls, they believed in also trying to change personal relationships between women and men. This is where the phrase 'the personal is political' comes from. What it means is that it is not enough to simply *say* that women and men should be equal, but those who believe this should try to make sure that within their relationships there is equality too. It means that women are treated with respect and dignity, that they are not put down, that things are organised so that they get their needs met too. If this were to happen, it was thought, then it would filter through society from the bottom up, and eventually make a contribution to the wider community. It was a good idea.

In this chapter we will be looking at a number of relationships and at what feminists have had to say about them. It is a difficult area to explore in some ways because it is really about unwritten rules, and about the complicated ways in which power relationships in society impact upon us personally.

There is great variety in the ways people relate to one another, but there is also a great deal of similarity. We are social animals and we learn about relationships, what to expect from them, and the right way to behave within them from our families initially, and later from society at large. This information comes from a number of sources. When we are young children we are given very clear messages, such as the importance of sharing toys (we rarely want to). We are taught the social rules very directly. Later, at school, we learn other rules less directly—the rules of the playground, perhaps. In adulthood we carry on learning—from our friends, from the movies we watch, from books we read, from the music we listen to, from our family, from our workmates. Through talking about relationships and, asking advice about relationships we learn what is appropriate and what is inappropriate behaviour. Again, it is informal, but this talking acts like a social glue in a way, because it creates a situation where, generally speaking, people abide by social rules. So let us have a look at the social rules.

Relationships with males

I said earlier that the power relationships in society at large have an important influence on private relationships. Given this fact, since the situation of women has improved considerably in the last fifty years, you could be forgiven for thinking that private relationships will have evened out too—and, to some extent, you would not be wrong. Just as society is always in a process of change, rules about relationships, and the relationships themselves, are too. But some things stay the same.

Fathers

According to psychologists, fathers tend to be the people who repre-sent authority and power in nuclear families (where a man and a woman live with their children). As children grow up, what happens is that boys want to be like their father and they learn, and copy, the behaviour of their fathers because they identify with him. Girls, on the other hand, grow up identifying with, and copying, their mothers. No great surprise there!

Sigmund Freud, the famous Austrian psychoanalyst, put another slant on it. He said that girls suffer from 'penis envy' because they make a connection between not having a penis and not having much power. He was not wrong! But feminists who have written about this in later years believe Freud *was* wrong to imagine girls are so envious, and that they spend much of their lives trying to get over this. They believe women are not just people with something missing, but people who possess amazing bodies which can even create life itself. They believe Freud overestimated the value and significance of having a penis, but was less wrong about the recognition that women had less power than men and wouldn't mind changing the situation.

But enough about psychology. It is thought by many feminists that within nuclear families things haven't changed very much and that one of the ways little girls learn to be obedient to men is that they learn it from their father, because he has much more authority than their mother. He is the one who decides the important things like how money is spent, the one who punishes children and the one who is the most keen on 'appropriate' gender behaviour—girls shouldn't climb trees and get dirty and boys shouldn't play with dolls or dress up.

A lot of modern families, particularly those influenced by feminist writing about these things, are attempting to change. Men are much more likely than ever before to be involved in the care of children. It is not seen so much as a 'woman's job'. There has been a lot written about how important it is (especially for boys) to have an involved father who is kind as well as tough, who has time for them and who cares for them in practical ways. It is seen as important because it gives boys a much better role model—one which equips them in later life to have more rewarding relationships.

So being caring has been added to the list of requirements of being a 'good father' now—largely because of the pressure from women. But does this mean they give away their role of authority? This doesn't seem to be happening. If it was to happen, it would mean that little girls were growing up in homes where they learned that women could be powerful and have the final say—'Wait until your mother gets home!'. But of course this is difficult for women who were taught themselves that men (their own fathers) were the ones with the power. So it is like a cycle which is hard to break. But maybe it is one worth breaking.

Lovers

This is the early point in any relationship where a man and a woman get to play out all the bits and pieces which go into a relationship. It is a minefield.

In years gone by it was all pretty easy—he paid, you went out to the movies or dinner or a party, and you certainly didn't get into bed for quite some time (if at all) before you tied the knot. Nowadays it is much more complicated because those social rules mentioned earlier have become much more loose. I guess as a mark of women's increasing economic independence from men, it is usual for women to pay for themselves. Furthermore, letting a man pay for you is interpreted, some would say, as a sign that you have offered more than just to go to the movies. Which is perhaps why young women like to use their own money—you are starting as equals and negotiate from there.

And then there is the question of *when* (not if) you have sex, get into bed, sleep with men and so on. Or not. The reason why it is an issue at all goes back to that 'sexual double standard' discussed in the first chapter. In the past, and within many groups of people today, different standards apply to men and women. For men, having sex is not thought to mean very much at all. Often it is called 'the horizontal handshake' as a (sort of) joke. Some theorists argue that having sex with women is a really important part of a man's sense of masculinity. In other words, it makes him feel more masculine and for some men, the more women he has slept with, the more masculine this makes him feel. Perhaps because of this, having sex with someone doesn't mean they necessarily have feelings for them (although they might, as well).

Women, on the other hand, are not thought well of if they have slept with a lot of men, although this might be changing now. But it doesn't make her feel more feminine to do so. In the past it was important for women to be monogamous (only have sex with one person at a time and preferably only with your husband) because this was the way men knew who their children were. So there was a great deal of social pressure for women to be more faithful than men. These ideologies are still around, which accounts for both the sexual double standard, and women's feelings about sex with men, which seem to be that it means some sort of commitment.

Younger feminist writers are changing these ideas. They seem to be saying that women's and men's sexual needs, and attitudes towards sex, are very similar. We will look at sexuality itself in a later chapter, but now it is just necessary to point out that, if anything, these old taboos are disappearing and being replaced by a much more equal and egalitarian attitude towards sex between men and women. I said 'attitude' because it doesn't necessarily follow that the relationships are more equal and egalitarian. And of course, young women are becoming less and less interested in getting married, which is what we turn to next.

Marriage and de facto relationships

Marriage rates are falling. More heterosexual couples are living together. Partnerships are lasting shorter and shorter amounts of time. Divorce is rising. About 80 per cent of divorces are sought by women. Why?

Perhaps the simplest reason is that women no longer have to be married, or be in a relationship to secure their economic welfare. In the past when women (if they worked at all) earned so little, it meant there were some very practical reasons to stay together—like a roof over your head and food on the table.

Nowadays, although women can suffer terribly after divorce financially (especially if they are single mothers) they can have the resources to look after themselves. Given this fact, the only real reason why couples stay together is the quality of the relationship. If it is no longer full of love, if he is unfaithful or you are, or if you are bored, there is not the social pressure nor the economic pressure for women to stay with men. And they don't.

So what happens to husbands and wives? Are they a dying breed? In the research done on the reasons for divorce, women most often say there is a lack of communication. They find that their husbands don't talk much and that they want to. In a recent book by Tom Morton called *Altered Mates. The Man Question*, he argues that when it comes to marriage, men and women have different expectations. He thinks men still see themselves as the breadwinner whose job it is to provide for his family, work hard, and to be the authority figure. As you can see, there is not much there about his wife apart from providing for her. Women, on the other hand, have changed in recent years, and what they seek in marriage is, above all, a loving and supportive relationship. He argues, then, that men see their partnerships as primarily economic and don't necessarily seek emotional fulfilment to any great extent, whereas women see their partnerships as primarily emotional. And, not surprisingly, these unspoken expectations often conflict.

In order to sustain the institution of marriage—or long-term heterosexual relationships—Tom Morton doesn't think that women should become more like men, but that men should become more like women. In other words, in a society where the 'breadwinner' role isn't really necessary because both partners work, the power which in the past automatically came with that role should be shared. Furthermore, if men want to keep women, they need to become more interested in communicating with them, being able to talk about their feelings and work on problems together. He thinks it is a case of men catching up.

Sons

As we've seen already, there has been quite a lot of feminist writing about the way we raise our children, because it is in these early years that patterns are set for life. So if boys are brought up in a home where they see their father tyrannise their mother or put her down, are encouraged to be aggressive, are taught not to talk about their emotions or show them ('big boys don't cry'), learn that being competitive and individualistic is good for boys, they will grow up as men with these qualities too. This is another example of grass-roots feminist work, which it is hoped will seep into wider society.

So feminists are dedicated to bringing up boys who show girls, and women, the respect they show other boys, and men. They also teach them qualities of nurturing, of talking about how they are feeling and learning to solve problems through speech rather than violence. It is not a matter of giving them dolls or other 'feminine' toys, but of teaching them through example. This is where the role modelling discussed earlier comes in. If their father wants, and has, a relationship of respect and equality with their mother, then as the boys mature, they will see this as quite normal and what they want too.

But here another factor emerges, as we have seen, because as the boy reaches school age he starts come into contact with other ideas, those around in society which say women are *not* as good as men and don't deserve so much. And as boys move into their teenage years, especially if they are heterosexual, they will be prey to the ideas—not only of their peers, but of wider society—about women's sexuality through such things as pornography, misogynist Hollywood movies and music which is derogatory to women. What kind of impact do these things have? Can they undo all the good work from the home? Well, I'm afraid the jury is out on this one. An educated guess would say that the good work is not undone, and that boys, like their sisters, live within a nexus of ideas. Their fundamental attitudes about women will not be changed completely, but might be altered. By how much it is difficult to say, largely because we have not seen a generation of men raised by feminists reach maturity yet. Watch this space!

Relationships with females

If I am right, and outside power relationships influence private and personal relationships, then relationships with women should be, on the whole, less fraught than those with males. This is because men have more power than women in society and this spills into everything. Although it is obvious that women are different from each other according to which economic class they come from, which sexual orientation they prefer, their age, their ethnic and racial identification and their physical abilities, they all share a similar position in relation to men—they are subordinate to them. In other words, just to take one example, it doesn't matter if a woman is rich or poor, she will always have less power than her partner, or any man who is as rich or as poor as she is. One of the results of this, it is argued, is that women have a sense of sisterhood with each other. You find this in women's toilets when the paper has run out and you are sharing what is left around, and at the supermarket checkout when one of you has a screaming child. There is the smile which says 'I understand you'.

More seriously, this sense of sisterhood can be a very sustaining thing. It helps in the workplace when you are in difficulty, it helps when a relationship has finished and she listens for hours, it helps when she has had a baby. If you are a woman, think for a moment of all the women who have helped you over the years (or even in recent days) and I'll bet there are a few.

Mothers

Just as boys identify with their fathers and want to be like them, little girls start out wanting to be like their mothers. That is why they like to dress up in their clothes and put on their make up—and act like them. Some psychologists have argued that growing up is much easier for girls than it is for boys for the simple reason that mothers are always around, and fathers rarely are, so little girls know the person they should grow up to be like. Because of this, girls don't have the same crises over femininity as boys have over masculinity where they are always in a state of trying to prove they are a 'man'. As teenagers, boys often try to establish their masculinity to their friends by drinking, driving, fighting and other masculine activities. Girls, on the other hand, seem much less concerned about proving they are a 'woman'. It appears to be a fact to them.

Obviously, most young women don't continue to copy their mothers! Indeed, in their teenage years they usually go out of their way to show they are the opposite of their mothers. Which might mean they will end up like their grandmothers—who their mothers rebelled against!! But, joking aside, teenage girls reject their mothers and all they stand for because they have to in order to establish who they are themselves—which is, of course, completely different!

But as adults, mothers and daughter are more often than not quite close. Perhaps not surprisingly, this closeness is increased according to how similar their lives are. Women with small children, for example, often report that their mothers are a huge support to them both physically and emotionally. Lesbian women whose mothers have also come out seek their wisdom. And so it goes on. It is not always the case, naturally, but more often than not, it is.

Lovers

It has been argued that the disparities in power experienced by men and women determine the personal relationships they have as well. Within heterosexual relationships, then, there are often negotiations about power too. The most extreme example of this might be domestic violence where a man chooses to inflict pain on his partner, and often his children too. Some psychologists believe this is because he feels a lack of power and tries to gain power through being violent. But most heterosexual women, at the other end of the spectrum, will have had experiences where they have been put down by the man they are in a relationship with, been made to feel a fool in front of others. Or maybe they have been told what they can do and what they can't do.

So when these external power relationships are not there, because the people in the relationship are both women, it seems rather obvious that the relationship might be a good deal more equal.

Many feminist writers who are also lesbians are interested in the ways in which personal and sexual relationships impact on wider society—again, 'the personal is political'. They argue that the quality of the relationships between women is better, due to the fact that they are equal partners. Also, we live in a patriarchy where it is very important to men to have access to women sexually and through this, men get to control women and to use them. Some argue that men use women to do everything from their cleaning to giving them emotional support when they need it. The point is that it is a one-way street because men do not give women emotional support in return very often. Well, you could argue about this all day long, but it is clear that there are links between heterosexual culture and patriarchy. In the next chapter we will be looking at sexuality itself and at some of the theory about why people have the desires they do and at the way sexuality in seen in contemporary society.

In recent years it seems that sexuality and sexual preferences (particularly among the middle classes) have become more fluid. Young people are less fixed as 'heterosexual' or 'homosexual' and move between these categories (or identities) more frequently than they used to. One of the results of this, arguably, is a proliferation of new cultural styles. What I mean by this is that, as we saw earlier, young women are experimenting with dress styles, with images of femininity which both defy and sometimes collude with traditional notions about sexuality. In other words, they might wear lipstick and high heels and short skirts, but this doesn't mean they are interested in men at all.

Finally, many lesbian feminists argue that lesbianism is crucial to the women's movement in that it means putting women first in your life rather than men, and that to do so means one is weakening patriarchy rather than strengthening it. They wonder how it can be that feminists, whilst being strongly resistant to patriarchy and all its trappings, and recognising the terrible power relationships between women and men, can make their lives with men, sleep with them and give them sustenance in various ways. Maybe the answer to this question lies in the realm of sexuality, which we will look at later.

Daughters

When it comes to raising daughters, as with sons feminists are interested in developing in them some of the qualities which are usually ironed out of young girls. As we have seen, young girls and boys are socialised very differently. Boys are socialised to be strong, physically fit, independent, unemotional and competitive, whereas girls are socialised to be caring, emotional, non-competitive, dependent, physically unconfident. Putting it differently, children are brought up to fulfil their gender roles. So boys are equipped with the know-how and confidence to take on male roles at home and in the work-place, and girls are equipped with the skills to be carers in various ways—both at home and in the workplace (more on this later).

The skills a boy is taught—self-confidence being an important one—enables him to do all sorts of things. The skills a girl is taught—caring for others' needs before their own being an important one—enables her to be an excellent communicator. But in terms of the big bad world a boy is better off. Many people have wondered why it is, for example, that women are reluctant to go into parliament or become barristers despite the fact they have the qualifications to do so. The answer might lie in the skills needed to do the job. You have to have enormous self-confidence and be very assertive to stand up in a courtroom and argue your point of view. Similarly, in parlia-ment, you have to be able to withstand constant criticism (including people yelling at you) and push your position strongly to win. This is not easy for a woman, because she has not been socialised in this way.

So feminists, as a rule, are keen to socialise their daughters in such a way as to give them the confidence and skills they need to achieve things—not only in the world of work, but in personal relationships too. Since self-esteem can be an elusive thing for girls and women, feminists try to ensure their daughters have it in spades. They try to teach them that their futures are not necessarily tied up to a man (or men) and that they can make choices about the sorts of relationships they get involved with. Some writers argue that in raising children we should try to develop in them 'androgyny', which means taking the best bits from masculinity (strength, independence, self-confidence) and the best bits from femininity (good social and communication skills, caring for others, emotional expressiveness) and combine them. If this were to happen, and both girls and boys were to be raised so that they have a balance of these characteristics, it is argued we would all be better off. One of the ways we would be better off is that men and women would be much more alike. No more 'men are from Mars, women are from Venus'. It would be more like 'we both come from Androgyny'!

But, like the situation with boys, we are watching and waiting to see whether girls raised by feminists turn out differently. My guess is that they will. Indeed, the young women in their twenties who are showing such energy and exploration and self-confidence may well be among them.

five

chapter

sexy feminism?:
sexuality

First, let me explain a few things. Sometimes people get the words 'sex' and 'sexuality' confused. 'Sex' really means your biological make-up—that is to say, whether you are a male or a female. The word 'sexuality', on the other hand, refers to sexual activity, or your sexual orientation (who you are sexually interested in). Another word which comes up in discussions about these matters is 'gender' and this is often confused with the word 'sex'. You will often find on forms that it asks for your 'gender' when it should be asking for your sex. In fact, gender really means the characteristics which your particular society thinks are appropriate for someone of your sex to have. As we have seen already, each society has pretty strict rules about what kinds of behaviour it is appropriate for men and women to indulge in. Some think men should be aggressive and others think it is OK for women to be so. Some cultures believe that men holding hands is quite normal, whereas others believe it is a sign that they may be gay and so disapprove of it. These things vary the world over, although practically every society has a strong belief that the way they do it is right, if not downright natural! The same is true of our society.

What is sexuality?

Well, the easy answer is what you do in bed (or out of it if you prefer!). One of the amazing things about human beings is that they seem to have an almost infinite array of sexual tastes. In other words, people like doing lots and lots of different sexual things. Nobody is quite sure why this is. Most commonly, people like to think that there is a strong link between sexual activity and reproduction (having babies) and that because of this connection, the only natural or proper way of having sex is in a way which achieves this end. Of course, some of the more conservative churches believe that conception is the only reason to have sex at all! I think they are fighting a losing battle on that one.

But this connection between sexual activity and conception seems a very weak one as we move towards the twenty-first century—and this is why. For heterosexuals, the arrival of the pill—the most reliable form of contraception to date—has meant that one can have sex throughout life without ever falling pregnant. So there is no necessary link there at all. Even if you want to have babies, of all the times you have sex, it might be only twice in your life that you conceive. In addition, because fertility rates are falling so much, reproductive technology (artificial conception) is becoming more and more a part of people's lives. In that case, sexuality is bypassed almost completely! Finally, for lesbians and gay men, the expression of their sexuality has nothing whatsoever to do with babies at all. But this doesn't mean that they don't have children.

Perhaps you can see from this that although people still sometimes perceive sexuality as something to do with children, for almost all of us, for 99.9 per cent of the time, it has nothing whatsoever to do with children. Instead it can be a leisure activity, just good fun, a way for couples to cement their relationship, a way to express part of yourself.

But having said that, our society has some very strong opinions about sexuality—what is on and what is not on. The most approved of kind of sexual expression is between women and men who are married. That is it. Sex outside marriage—not so good. Gay sex is seen as the work of the devil by conservatives (who luckily are dying out). Sex between young people is a bit of a no-no. And so on.

The point about this is that although people think that sexuality is natural (well, a certain kind is), there is no doubt at all that it is a kind which is supportive of the status quo. That is why it is so heavily promoted everywhere you look and in everything you read. All the Hollywood movies you have ever seen (with a very few exceptions) will be about heterosexuality. These movies teach people how to operate sexually. Because people are usually sexual in private, we learn how to have sex and what to do most often through movies, TV, and sometimes through fiction. They give both men and women the same message. Women should be beautiful and passive and alluring. Men should be virile, in control and strong. In the act itself, the woman is passive and the man is active. If another model is given where the woman is sexually predatory, keen on sex, and won't do as she is told (for example in *Fatal Attraction*, *Disclosure*, *Basic Instinct* or any other Michael Douglas film), she gets what is coming to her and it isn't very nice. Watching movies like these is the way we learn about how to behave sexually, what to do. This is true for both straight and gay people. So a norm is established and the more you waver from that norm as an individual, the more you are seen as a deviant by society.

Another example of the way these ideas are evident in our society is when women are murdered. At the time of writing, there is a serial killer on the loose and he has killed a number of women (I feel safe using the word 'he' because there has never been a female serial killer). In the newspaper reports about this, it is said over and over again, both explicitly and implicitly as if it were very, very important, that the murdered women were 'decent'. In other words, although they had been at a nightclub on their own, they were not seen as whores (gasp!) and this makes the crimes committed against them all the worse. Of course, if they were less 'decent' according to the journalist's code of morality, their deaths would not be seen as so sad.

It is perhaps clear now that sexuality is something which is deeply affected by the society in which we live, and cannot be seen as something 'natural' (as if society had no impact upon it). Many feminist writers have argued that there is a serious reason why the 'naturalness' of sexual behaviour is promoted so heavily—because it is a key way in which patriarchy is maintained, and, of course, if it is 'natural' then it cannot be changed. It would be a bit like trying to change someone's sense of humour or their accent. But we know from other cultures that our notions about sexuality, and our ways of expressing it, are not 'natural' but are socialised into us, and the more you conform to the most approved style of sexual behaviour (heterosexual, woman passive and alluring, man in control and virile and hopefully married to the woman), the more status you are given in society. Or, perhaps it is more accurate to say that if you *don't* conform, you are not approved of and you receive the least status.

Sexual categories

You might have noticed that I have been using some sexual categories—straight, gay, heterosexual, homosexual. There are also bisexuals, transvestites, transsexuals, swingers, sadomasochists, people who buy sex from sex workers and so on and so on.

One of the best writers about the way we have looked at sex in the twentieth century is a French theorist called Michel Foucault. He said that modern societies are completely obsessed by sex, and he argued that our society has been so since the Victorian era. I think he is right about the obsession. When you look at other cultures, and

Foucault suggests that prior to the Victorian era it was the case in our society, they see sex as a normal activity which adults engage in. A bit like eating or going to the toilet. But what developed was a situation where sexuality became an area of life in which other impulses or desires were played out.

One example of this might be a desire for a change or excitement or power or emotional security. If you think about it, these might all be at play in a sexual relationship (or the decision to leave one relationship for another—or to stay). But they have nothing to do with the sex and everything to do with the meaning given to it, and to the relationship the sex produces. In other words, sexuality is a field where desires or impulses about other things come to the fore.

I know a man in his forties who was ripe for a mid-life crisis. He had had a long relationship with his female partner. He was slightly bored with his life and had gone through a phase where he was seriously contemplating being unfaithful to his partner because (he realises now) he wanted more risk in his life, and more excitement. But instead of destroying his relationship, and large parts of his life alongside it, he decided to fulfil this need for risk and excitement through other means. So he took up life-threatening sports—sky diving, white water rafting, hang gliding and all that sort of thing. These sports sorted him out. He is a man of insight, obviously, and he recognised that the essence of his desire wasn't for sex with someone new, but was for danger, and he could fulfil that in a way which protected what was most important to him in the long term—his relationship with his wife and with his children.

Michel Foucault, who was a historian, argues that as the obsession with sex grew, so did sexual categories like 'homosexual' and 'heterosexual', in contrast to previous times, where who you had sex with and how was no more meaningful than what you had for dinner last night. In our era, the 'who?' and 'how?' questions become extremely important because they are seen as defining the 'truth of you'. And so it was that the categories 'homosexual' and 'heterosexual' came to be invented and used. It must be said that this categorising of sexual orientations is directed much more at gay people than it is at straight. In other words, if you prefer your sex with people of the *same* sex, this is thought to define everything about you—what you eat, who you socialise with, where you go, what music you listen to, which movies you like. It is argued by some writers that the reason for this categorisation—particularly as it is applied to gay people—is

another way of establishing a norm and a deviancy. In other words, by stereotyping gay people ('they are like this and this') they are seen as deviants and heterosexual people are seen as 'normal' and part of this being normal is that they are so full of variety that they cannot be typed.

Yet again we return to the idea that sexual expression and power relationships in society are closely entwined. Gay people are threatening to the *status quo* (no matter what they do for a living) because they do not participate in the man/woman, strength/passivity roles. Gay women are not interested in looking after, and servicing, men's needs and gay men don't want to become providers for women and have children with them. And so on. So this lack of interest is a worry to—shall we say—the old fashioned section of the community because they think it shows that gender roles are starting to break down and civilisation, as we know it, will end. Or maybe civilisation will begin.

Feminists on sexuality

It must be said that feminism is not seen as a sexy pursuit. Now why is this? I would say that the answer has already been outlined in a way. Where sexuality is connected strongly to particular gender roles (you know, the one where the woman is just plain good-looking and passive, and the man comes on to her very energetically), and as we have seen, these gender roles are quite crucial to wider power relations in society in which women are subordinated, it is likely that people who want to do something about that will happily go along with whatever helps to support it. And that is why feminism is not seen as 'sexy'.

From the beginning of second wave feminism, also, writers have looked in some detail at the connections between our sexual power structures, and those in society at large. Some radical feminists, for example, have argued that male sexuality poses a clear and present danger to women; that it is cruel and unusual. Of particular concern is the act of penetration because they see it as unnecessary, but also as both a symbol of oppression and, indeed, an acting out of oppression. The most extreme example of this, of course, is rape. But in any case of penetration, either forced or accepted willingly, they believe that women have been programmed to put up with it. This point of view does women a disservice, I think, because it perceives them as (obviously) easy to brainwash and not really knowing what is good for them. What it cannot accommodate is that many women like penetration. You can argue about why that is, but they just do and they do not see it as an act of oppression or of anything else much.

Saying things like 'penetration is an oppression' is seen as so outrageous that it gets a huge amount of attention in the media and in conversations. The degree of attention perhaps indicates just how important it is to our society. It is meaningful, in other words. According to society, penetration *is* sex. But for many people this is far from the truth.

Pornography

Another sexual issue which feminists have spoken about is pornography. Pornography is sexually explicit film or photographs which focus on women. It makes massive amounts of money. Naomi Wolf in *The Beauty Myth* claims that in the USA the pornography industry makes more than twice as much as the music industry and Hollywood movies *combined*. That is a great deal of money. Some pornography is very expensive because it features acts which are illegal, or are on the edge of being illegal, such as sex with children or animals, or very violent pornography, which might account for how much money it makes.

Many radical feminists believe pornography is very bad indeed for women because it circulates a view of women—as sex objects—which helps men to think of women in this way and so to dehumanise them. It helps them to treat women in the real world with contempt.

I went to a seminar about pornography once where the man who runs the company which produces the majority of pornographic magazines was speaking. His line was quite predictable—'men like pornography. We make it for men. It is harmless'. An older woman stood up and asked him if he would be happy to see his wife or daughter in one of his harmless magazines. The speaker went ballistic and started to shout. He said it was an appalling question and that he would not answer it, and so on. The point about his anger is that he couldn't bear the thought of someone he cared about being in one of his magazines. He couldn't even cope with the thought of it! And there is a simple reason for that, which is that they are not good for women. Not those who appear in them nor women in the wider community.

Pornographic imagery is spreading further and further into our lives. It is used in TV advertising, on billboards, in magazines. There are places where you can see pornography come alive—in table top dancing venues where women who are naked (how can I put it?!) let men give them a gynaecological examination. Of a kind. Strippers and topless barmaids are proliferating. It is arguable that the reason for all this activity is that we have got used to pornography being all around us. We see it everyday. We see it everywhere.

You don't have to be a genius to figure out that this is not good. Pornography does not promote healthy images of women. They don't seem like real people with feelings and needs. It makes them look like collections of body parts about which men can fantasise doing things to. One of the important things to consider when looking at the impact of pornography is whether these pictures remain as images in people's minds, or whether they are acted out in real life, whether they change the way men treat women. It's the same question which is asked about the impact of violent or pornographic video and computer games. The jury is out on the answer because the connection is firstly a difficult one to firmly establish and secondly, the *degree* of the connection is a difficult one to determine. Nevertheless, it seems to me that it is possible to argue that pornography serves the purposes of men rather than women, and does not offer anything useful to society at all and just might offer some really bad things. We'd be much better off without it.

Pornography seems to increase when women have more rights. So, in a situation where women seem to be improving their situation in many ways, perhaps you should not be surprised at this increase. Maybe it puts women in their place. Or reminds them where their place is. And it also provides men with the material to fantasise about having power over women in a very private and personal way. Yuk.

It might be that it is because feminists have pointed out why pornography exists and some of the impact it has on people's lives, and spoken about sexual matters as they are, which add to the perception that feminism is, somehow, anti-sex. That it is unsexy. One result of such name-calling is that young women are less likely, because of this, to feel comfortable aligning themselves with feminism. Again, it is social death and likely to put men off you for life! Not so.

Girl power

Young women writing about sexuality take a very different perspective from the one which suggests that women are brainwashed and victimised; that all penetration is rape of a kind. Instead, they view women as active participants in sexual encounters. They see them as capable of being sexual predators. They see them as able to have sex without emotion. They see them as having a strong sexual appetite.

In a sense, this viewpoint is very close to the way we see men's sexuality and what these young women seem to be saying is that men and women *are* very alike in these matters nowadays. This is certainly the impression you would get sauntering past any magazine rack: 'One night stands: A survival guide', 'How to get that man', 'The orgasm that lasts 179 times longer. Come and get it', 'Fat or thin? Who has the better time in bed?', 'Oral sex. Why you are getting more than ever'. It doesn't mean that young women do see themselves like this, or act like this, but it is interesting that the media want them to. Let's face it, it is long way from knitting patterns and advice about how to get stains off clothes or how to apply mascara!

If earlier feminist writing about sex was done at a time when women really were much less powerful than men and this was reflected also in their sexual encounters, then as we move into the twenty-first century, and as women gain power in the public world and hopefully within themselves as well, we might well find that sexually they find their feet as well (if you get my meaning!). All the young women who are into girl power might well dress up to the nines, but this doesn't mean they can be taken for a ride. They feel powerful and perhaps then they are. And as the society in which they live comes to expect young women and young men to share the same sexual desires and needs, they will come to have them. This is because societies determine how you see your sexuality and, as a result, what your sexuality is like. Not nature and not anything else.

six
chapter

well women:
health and vitality

Health is a funny thing. We all seem to be chasing it in one way or another. Actually, women seem to chase it more than men do. They go to doctors more than men. Advertisements for products related to 'health'—everything from breakfast cereals to shampoo—are aimed at women rather than men. This chapter will look at why this is and at the way(s) we think about health. 'Health' has to be one of the most overused words this century!

What is 'health'?

Perhaps the most obvious answer to this question is that to be 'healthy' means not to be ill. But it goes further than this because health, according to popular understanding, is something no one really has and yet everyone (in industrialised societies) strives for! In industrialised societies people are extremely healthy compared to non-industrialised societies such as those in Africa, Asia, Central and Southern America, the Pacific region and parts of Eastern Europe since the fall of the Eastern bloc. They are also much healthier than at any time in the past. The main reason for this is that those fortunate enough to live in these places have a good food supply, fresh water and a sanitation system which removes sewage. In addition, because of inoculation against the major diseases which used to kill us, such as measles, polio, tuberculosis and so on, our live expectancies have risen and we anticipate having (for the most part) a life free of major illness.

Because of these (to us) simple things, it is possible to say that most people in industrialised societies live in a state of health. This seems almost an outrageous thing to say because we are living in a time in which people believe the opposite to be true. Exercise (doing some), nutrition (eating vegetables and fruit, drinking water), lifestyle (getting enough sleep, not using drugs, drinking 'excess' amounts of alcohol, smoking cigarettes, having unsafe sex or not using sunscreen) are the messages which seem to assail us from practically every vantage point. I'm not suggesting that this is necessarily a bad thing, simply that it is a peculiar thing. It is also peculiar that health issues have a higher impact on women than they do on men, both in terms of women's concerns about health, given the fact that they tend to live much longer than men and suffer less from the main causes of premature death than men do, and in terms of the attention which the medical profession pay to women. Let's look at some of the reasons feminists have offered for these things.

A history of health and healing

We are so used to thinking about our health as being linked to doctors that it is easy to forget that they are quite a recent invention, and that the growth of the medical profession has been very strongly connected with issues to do with gender.

Before the rise of science in the West women were responsible for healing. It is doubtful if there was such a thing as health at the time. There was illness and not-illness. Women were pretty much responsible for getting rid of illness. This is true even today if you think about it because women are, by and large, the people who care for the young, the elderly, the disabled. Often this is in a paid capacity. But when it comes to maintaining the health of families, both at times of illness and when all are well, it is women who do this. They even do it for friends and for people in their wider community. It is not unusual, for example, for women to cook meals for new mothers, to help out with sick children if a mother has to work. And so on.

But prior to the age of science, there were women in most communities who had a designated role to do this. They were called 'wise women' and they healed people using many of the herbs, teas and tinctures which are being rediscovered now. They also often acted as midwives.

These were the women, according to many feminist writers, who were killed in their millions in Western Europe for witchcraft. The men who organised their deaths (most often being burned alive at the stake) argued that they were doing the work of the devil because it was God's will that people suffered illness. In other words, they thought that these women, who were mostly single and, because of this, lived outside the patriarchal family system, were in league with the devil and should therefore die. They had various revolting ways of torturing and then killing them which are too gruesome to go into (see reading list at the end of the book!)

Following this, there was a shift, in that men became involved in health, and through science medicine was developed. There were a lot of wars around this time and it was through war that men learned surgery. At first, it was barbers who did it because they were the ones with the sharp instruments. In England, barbers still have the red and white striped poles outside their shops which symbolise blood and bandages!

With the growth of science came the growth in medicine, the medical schools and the regulation of a profession which had been, until then, something people learned from their elders. Soon you needed a qualification to act as a doctor. Not surprisingly, it was men rather than women who got to go to medical school—women were banned from them. These days things have changed, luckily, and around half of those entering medical school are women. Despite this, the medical profession is a male dominated profession in many ways. In terms of numbers (perhaps for historical reasons) they tend to dominate all the specialties. But feminists have also argued that a particularly Western male view of the world dominates medicine—one where mind and body are not necessarily seen as connected, and where people are not treated as people but as collections of symptoms and body parts. It means that the human body is seen a bit like an engine—if there is a faulty part you replace it and all should be well. Other medical traditions, on the other hand, see the body as a complicated and connected system, so that you cannot treat one part of it without affecting other parts. Many writers see this more holistic approach as a more female approach, even though it is practised by both men and women in other parts of the world and seems to be increasingly influencing even Western medicine.

The last twenty years have seen a growth in interest in different ways of viewing health and treating illness, and many people argue that this is a reclaiming of pre-scientific, feminine traditions. There has been a resurgence of interest in homoeopathy (the use of plant extracts which mimic the illness in order to provoke the body's natural defences) and in such things as bach flower remedies, naturopathy and some Asian medical techniques such as acupuncture. All these forms of treatment rely on the notion that the body has an integrated system in which the treatment of one part inevitably affects other parts. They are also, arguably, 'unscientific' in the sense that they have not always been subjected to the rigorous testing which orthodox treatment or drugs have undergone. But this doesn't mean that they don't work.

The medical profession is scathing about these remedies, or practices, on the whole. Indeed, it spends a good deal of time and money in trying to make sure that those who treat patients using them cannot get professional recognition. Some argue that the reason for this is a pretty simple one—the medical profession is just defending its turf. It doesn't want competition in the marketplace. Others, however, believe the reasons for its hostility go deeper. They believe that medicine is a deeply patriarchal industry and its actions are about maintaining patriarchy as much as it is about making a (very good) living. So let us look at the evidence for such a claim!

Medical views of women's bodies

It is argued that the medical profession, because it is dominated by men, and has a particularly masculine set of values underpinning it, tends to see women as a problem. They see women's bodies as unusual compared to men's bodies which they see as the norm. An example of this point of view in practice is the way in which drugs are tested. Deborah Saltman, a professor of medicine at Sydney University, reports that female animals are never used to test drugs such as those for cancer or heart disease (which obviously affect both women and men) because females are seen as 'unreliable'. They are unreliable because they have hormonal fluctuations which males don't have. In other words, males are viewed as reliable or normal, and females are subsequently positioned as the opposite. You might be wondering about the impact of these drugs on women. As well you might.

Another example of the medical profession's perspective on women is evident, it is argued, through a process called 'medicalisation'. What this means is that normal and natural experiences such as birth or menopause are increasingly being defined as problems—almost as illnesses—which require medical attention. There are many examples of normal bodily experiences which have been redefined in this way (often experiences which relate to the female reproductive system) leading to an increase in the influence of medicine in our lives.

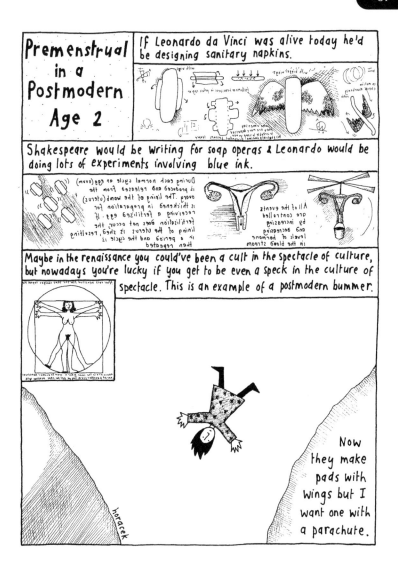

Pre-menstrual syndrome

Some women experience such things as fluid retention and mood swings in the days before they menstruate. But many don't. In the last few years, though, PMS has been not only named and partly defined, but has become almost a condition which is treated by doctors through a variety of drugs, often the contraceptive pill which stops you ovulating and menstruating (naturally) altogether.

There are also a huge range of treatments available from 'natural' sources such as Evening Primrose Oil, vitamins and diuretics.

Menopause

An area of huge activity currently. Menopause is a natural process which occurs when a woman is in her late forties or early fifties and her reproductive system is starting to wind down. In the past it was seen as something unproblematic and natural. But today the opposite is true because it has been refined by the medical profession as a process which requires medical intervention. Hormone Replacement Therapy has been developed to 'treat' menopause. This therapy involves women taking synthetic oestrogen and progesterone—the hormones which wind down—and is said to not only 'relieve the symptoms' of menopause (hot flushes, night sweats, lethargy), but offer women protection against osteoporosis and heart disease. I heard a specialist on the radio the other day saying that he hoped in twenty years that ALL menopausal women will be on it. Why?!

Birth

This is perhaps the issue which has received the most attention in both the popular press and in feminist writing because it is probably the most extreme example of medicalisation. At the risk of being boring, it should be stated that birth is a natural event which can be done extremely successfully without any medical intervention at all in over 90 per cent of cases.

But the process of pregnancy and birth has been recast as one in which medical intervention is necessary to ensure a healthy mother and baby. Not so! It is true that the death rates have fallen dramatically this century since birth in hospital became the norm, but it has been argued that this has as much to do with good nutrition and women's general health status as it has with obstetrics. Nowadays, in hospital, the birth process is highly medicalised. This means that women are given drugs and have procedures done to them which take away their natural ability to give birth. One of these procedures is induction, where labour is artificially brought on using either an intravenous drug called oxytocin or through 'breaking the waters' or through pessaries. Births are induced for a number of reasons, not least among these being convenience for the doctors.

Induced labour tends to be quicker and more painful than natural labour—often because the baby is not quite ready to emerge. Because of this, painkillers are used more frequently. A popular painkiller is the epidural which is injected into your spine (ouch!) and numbs you from the waist downwards. This means you can't feel the contractions, which means that it can be difficult to know when to push. Without an epidural, you just know. What happens often after this is that the baby is delivered with forceps—an instrument rather like a big pair of tongs—because it doesn't descend on its own because the pushing mechanism has been interfered with. The baby is pulled down the birth canal by the head with these. At delivery, it is common for women to have an episiotomy where you are cut from the vagina to the anus. This facilitates the head coming out quickly. An alternative to this is just to ease the head out slowly.

This birth process involves what has been called a 'cascade of intervention' where one procedure leads almost inevitably to another (the induction to the epidural to the forceps to the episiotomy). Most of the time none of this is necessary but it has become pretty standard in modern hospitals. So the question must be asked 'why?'. Most feminist writers believe it is because modern medicine wants to take power away from women and put it in the hands of the male obstetricians (for most are men). Even the usual position for giving birth (lying on your back) is one designed to enable the obstetrician to see what is going on, whereas being on all fours or squatting means that gravity does the job much better.

In recent times there has been a birth movement which has campaigned to change these practices and return birth to a much more natural state. Today, for example, it is possible to give birth in birthing centres where you are attended by midwives rather than doctors and where medical intervention doesn't occur unless there is a major problem. These centres were established after pressure from women, particularly feminist women, who wanted to empower women to take control over their own births because they believed that doing so made a massive difference to their confidence and ultimately to their health after birth and to their relationships with their children.

Infertility

In the past infertility was seen as a fact of life. People had no children for a variety of reasons and this was just one of them. These days, however, it is seen as both a social and medical catastrophe. It is a social catastrophe because there is a great deal of pressure for women to have children (perhaps because fewer young women want to?). It is seen as a medical catastrophe because a functioning reproductive system is viewed as a key part of women. Infertility is no longer seen as a barrier to having children because they have developed a number of methods to create children artificially.

This is a difficult area, because there is no doubt that women do have strong desires to have children. Where this desire comes from is a controversial question. Some argue it is instinctive but this is not easy to prove given the cultural and individual variations. Others argue the desire come from a society which defines women in terms of their childbearing roles. Having children is seen as a feminine thing to do. A heterosexual thing to do.

In any case, there are now numerous medical procedures designed to enable women with fertility problems to have babies. Notice the lack of procedures for men! Most of these procedures involve large amounts of time, money and drugs of which no one really knows the long-term effects.

Perhaps the most famous one is invitro-fertilisation. This is where a sperm and egg are joined outside the woman's body and then placed in her womb. They get her eggs by giving her superovulatory drugs which mean she produces many eggs at ovulation instead of just one. Then they 'harvest' them. After fertilisation they put a number inside her uterus and hope at least one implants. Sometimes many do which is why twins, triplets and quads are not uncommon for IVF mothers. But perhaps more concerning of all is that the failure rate of IVF is incredibly high. Of a hundred women who undergo it, less than ten will end up with a baby. Pregnancy rates are higher, but so is miscarriage.

But what about the woman whose 'infertility' is a result of the fact that she is post-menopausal? No worries! Using fertility drugs, women in their forties, fifties and even sixties can be made fertile again! And it happens. A sixty-four year old woman in Italy gave birth recently.

There are three main concerns about all this. The first is an attitudinal concern. Is it not possible for women *not* to have children— even when they are old? Of course, no one is forcing them to do it, but their very desire to do it is, it seems to me, a result of the emphasis in our society on women and reproduction. Secondly, as I said earlier, no one knows what the results of using all these drugs and techniques will have (physically) on future generations and it might well be that they do affect them. Thirdly, it seems that these medical procedures are advancing so quickly, that we barely have time to take a breath! There is surrogacy (where one woman carries a child for another which might or might not have genetic material from the birth mother), there is embryo experimentation on the embryos created for IVF which are surplus, there is the use of bits of embryos for curing other medical conditions (theoretically diabetes and Parkinson's disease being among them), there is cutting bits off embryos which are going to be implanted if they are carrying genes which are unwanted (in theory genes for nasty diseases, but it could be anything), there is sex selection of embryos (nearly all societies prefer boys to girls, which leads to the drastic imbalances in the numbers of the sexes we are seeing in China, for example, where they have a one child policy and they all want sons), and finally human cloning is on the agenda now where it is possible to reproduce people without sperm who are exact genetic replicas of their mothers. And so it goes on.

Aside from the ethical, legal and religious issues wrapped up in all this technology there is the simple fact that it is technology aimed at women. Even when, for example, a man has defective sperm and the woman is very fertile, it is she who goes through IVF. Perhaps you can figure out why this is.

Obesity

The last example of medicalisation is not about reproduction, but about our bodies nevertheless. Gone are the days where people came in all shapes and sizes. Gone are the days of voluptuous women. Obesity has been discovered as an illness.

Firstly, it was defined. This meant deciding what the 'correct' weight for people of particular heights was. Next, people who varied from this were categorised as having a medical problem. Then came the cure. The cure has been changed from dieting and taking appetite suppressants (amphetamines, in fact) to eating particular food and exercising. In addition, of course, there are all the industries discussed in Chapter three which connect with the medical profession in various ways—the dieting industry, the cosmetic surgery industry and so on. They are all dedicated to both persuading people that their 'natural' body shape is wrong and that they should change it.

'But' I hear you cry, 'Being overweight is unhealthy!'. This sounds good, but it is vague. What does 'unhealthy' mean? What does 'overweight' mean'? The fact is that unless you are *extremely* overweight so that you cannot really exercise, or your organs are working far too hard, being 'overweight' is no problem at all. On the other hand, dieting so much that your nutritional levels are under par and you have stopped menstruating is a health risk. But you don't hear much about that, do you?

But there is a gender issue at work here as well since men are more often 'overweight' than women, yet women think they are overweight (even when they are not) and are subjected to all the propaganda about weight, and doing something about it, which is not aimed at men.

Perhaps you can see from these examples that medicalisation—the increasing involvement of medicine in people's lives and the redefining of quite normal, natural states as medical problems—is something which affects women a great deal more than it affects men. It seems to have two sources. The first is money. The medical industry (for that is what it is) is constantly on the lookout for new markets, new problems, new syndromes and conditions, which drug companies can develop drugs for and medical professionals can be involved in treating. The second source is one which cannot be avoided—since much of this activity is directed at women rather than at men, and is linked directly with primarily social as well as medical issues—the idea must be entertained that medicalisation is a form of social control on women. It defines them as a problem and medicine is increasingly involved in their lives.

Be wise about doctors. Be wise about what they say to you. Think about what you are diagnosed as having, about what drugs you are taking. Find out what you can about everything and make intelligent decisions. You are in charge of your body and you know it better than anyone else.

Have a look at some of the manuals recommended at the end of this book which are designed to help you make informed decisions about your own health and your own body. And remember, use your brain and use your body too.

chapter
seven

beyond the glass
ceiling: work

O ne of the first things which second-wave feminists wanted to do something about was their working conditions. At the time, men and women were paid different amounts of money for doing the same work. The reasoning behind this was that men had families to support (and women didn't?!) so they needed more money. The other linked issue was that, like today, men and women worked in different areas and even when they worked in the same field, they were not often in the same jobs.

The facts of the matter were that men were much better off than women—and they still are today despite all the effort that has been put into changing this situation. In this chapter we are going to have a quick canter through some of the issues relating to work and to gender which have been at the forefront of the battle(s) in the workplace.

What kinds of work do women do? And why?

In a lot of feminist writing about work, they divide the world into two spheres—the 'public' sphere and the 'private' sphere. The public sphere refers to the big world out there. It involves the world of education, politics, the law, medicine, industry, the media, the union movement, trades of all kinds, the computer industry and so on. In other words, all the workplaces which are outside the home.

The private sphere, on the other hand, is taken to mean the domestic world where all the 'reproduction', rather than the 'production', takes place. By 'reproduction', I mean all the background tasks which are undertaken in order that people can go out into the workforce in the first place. These can include washing, ironing and repairing clothes and linen, cleaning, buying food, preparing and cooking food, buying clothes and household items, house maintenance (such as painting and repairing both the house and its furnishings), looking after children, educating children, caring for the sick and elderly, looking after pets, answering phones and so on.

Having made a list of the parameters of these two spheres, you might have noticed something already—men tend to be located primarily in the public sphere and women primarily in the private sphere. Even if women work full-time, they tend to do the home and people maintenance as well. This is what is often referred to as the 'double-shift', where women do a day's work and return home to start on all the other stuff. Which generally men don't do.

But it goes further than this, because although the rates of women working (even those with small children) have gone up dramatically over the last thirty years, women tend to work in the areas which involve the tasks that they undertake at home. Consequently, they work in hospitality, childcare, teaching, nursing, social work, cleaning, in the retail sector, as psychologists. And very few work as engineers, as architects, as academics, journalists, plumbers or electricians.

Once more comes that annoying question—why?

Well, very simply, it might well be because women want to do work with people rather than with things. They want to work in areas where they feel comfortable (which often means working with other women rather than with men) and they feel comfortable doing jobs which echo their domestic roles. Obviously, few women would think of it in this way, but the facts remain. And once again, we might well look at the way we are socialised as young children for some clues about why it might be that males and females fit into male and female worlds of work so well.

At the risk of repeating myself, it is important to say that girls are raised in a way which makes them have certain skills. Perhaps the most important of these for our purposes here are 'people' skills. They are good at communicating, at relating to people, and they tend to enjoy this (although there are always exceptions to this, of course!). Because of the way they are socialised they enjoy work which uses these sorts of skills—skills which help people. Boys, on the other hand, are raised in quite a different manner. They are taught about spatial skills, how to fix things, how to be confident enough to tackle arguments, how to assert themselves in a variety of situations. It is also arguable that they are raised with the expectation that they are going to have a lifetime of work, and that it is work (rather than home life and family life) which will be important to them. This might be why unemployment can be so devastating to men. Obviously, there are always the financial problems which arise with unemployment, but many men report that it is the blow to their self-esteem which is the most difficult to deal with because they have built their image of themselves as a worker at a particular occupation and to have this taken away wrecks their sense of themselves. I am not suggesting that women don't go through some of the same problems, but that they can be offset by their sense of themselves as a mother, a wife, a daughter—by their relationships with others which are important to them and give them a sense of their place in the world.

So we can see that work can be seen as having different meanings for men and women, and that men and women tend to do different kinds of work. You might not think that this is very important. Does it matter that women have the skills for 'people' work and like doing it? That men have the personal and professional skills to be barristers or surgeons, journalists or plumbers?

I think it matters for two reasons. Firstly, if you think about it, the kind of work which men do in the public domain is the kind of work which propels our community. They are the ones making the laws, writing about politics (even being politicians!), teaching in universities, running the union movement, the medical profession and the media. These are the areas of work which really determine the kind of society we live in, and the ideas about that which we all have.

Perhaps it is time for a classic quote from an early feminist text by Kate Millett called *Sexual Politics* which was published in 1969:

> . . . our society, like all other historical civilisations is a patriarchy. The fact is evident at once if one recalls that the military, industry, technology, universities, science, political office, and finance—in short, every avenue of power in the society, including the coercive force of the police, is entirely in male hands (p. 25).

Although if Kate Millett was writing this now she might leave out the word 'entirely' (more on this later) and add the words 'the media', it still remains a fact that these avenues of power which run the society are heavily dominated by men. This matters because it means that women don't, in the end, have much say in how things are run. If they did, it might well be that they would do things differently. Who knows?

The second reason why it matters that men and women do such different work is probably quite an obvious one—the work which men do pays more. All those jobs in the public sphere are much more highly paid than those in the private sphere (jobs which are similar to those done at home). Indeed, the more private the job, the less it is paid. Perhaps childcare workers are a good example of this. They have to study for three years to get qualified and they learn about a huge range of things such as child development, child psychology, nutrition, art, first-aid, language development and so on. Despite this expertise their wages are very low indeed when compared to other occupations for which you have to study for a similar amount of time. It is a job with low status. The reason for this low status is probably both because it is a job undertaken almost wholly by women, and because it is work which women do at home for free. This might be illogical, but the ideas behind it are those which relegate women, and what they do, to second-class status.

Nursing is a good example of the way in which the status of 'women's work' can change. In the past nurses were trained in hospitals, they were almost all women and had little status. This has changed now with the increase in numbers of men entering what has become a profession. Nurses are now required to do a degree at a university and their hospital training has become only a small part of their overall education. Perhaps because of this, and because of the increasing numbers of men entering the field, nurses are enjoying a good deal more professional status. It seems to be that women carry low status with them wherever they go whilst men carry high status wherever they go. Weird but true.

So 'women's work' pays less, but there are other problems with it too. Women tend to work in areas which are both low-paid and also insecure. They are less likely than men to have permanent jobs, instead they are on contracts or (even worse) are casual workers who are picked up and dumped whenever the employer feels like it. Of course, workers in industries like the hospitality industry (which is female dominated) are prey to this casualisation of labour more than other areas of work.

One of the big problems with casual work is that it is very difficult to maintain a relationship with the union which protects you because you change jobs a lot. Secondly, doing casual work means you are not entitled to the benefits which come with permanent employment such as sick leave, maternity leave, annual leave and payment into superannuation schemes. Further down the track, having little or no superannuation can mean you are facing old age with much fewer resources than people who have had permanent employment despite the fact that you have worked for the same number of years and maybe even earned a similar wage!

So you can see from this broad overview that there are a lot of issues to do with gender in the workplace even today, and that many of these issues have been around for a long time. But perhaps it is time to look at some of the strategies which have been employed in order to make the workplace one which treats men and women more equally and tries to redress the power imbalances.

Representation in the avenues of power

We need to look at this first because people often seem to be under the misguided belief that things are changing. That women are becoming more and more senior. Let me tell you that this is not the case—no matter how much we all might want it to be. No matter which occupation you want to look at, whether it be anything from medicine to politics to the judiciary, you will find far fewer women than men in these prestigious fields and even fewer in their higher echelons. In other words, there is a glass ceiling—a barrier you can see, and see through, but which you seem unable to break through.

The reasons for this are complex. If you look at medicine and law, which are two of the most highly-paid and influential occupations, the picture is not a good one, although it might look good on the surface. Firstly, females are achieving the very high marks in their secondary education which they need to get into law school and medical school at the same rate as their male counterparts. Secondly, they are graduating from these schools with law and medical degrees at the same rate as men (in other words, they are not dropping out). But it is what happens to them after that which is problematic.

Both these fields have quite a clear hierarchy. In medicine it goes like this—General Practitioner (GP), then Consultant (Specialist) (there are other levels of seniority during training). In law, being a solicitor is followed by being a barrister which is followed by being a Queen's Council (QC) which is followed by being a judge. Being a judge on the High Court is probably as far as you can go. Now, when people cheerfully say that equal numbers of men and women go into and finish law and medical school, they often forget to add that women, by and large, never get very far. They don't become specialists and judges, they stay being General Practitioners and solicitors. Likewise, although there are women academics working in universities, they stay as casual tutors and rarely ever become Professors or Vice-Chancellors. In the private sector you will very rarely find a woman on a board of directors.

Feminists have pondered upon these things for a long time. Before the changes to the law we will look at next, it was quite legal and acceptable to openly discriminate against women and simply refuse them the job or the promotion, but you can't do this legally any more, so other explanations for these gender differences in holding powerful jobs have to be found. Some writers think the reason for this state of affairs is something we have touched on already—the public/private split. Because women are seen as the ones responsible for not only childbearing, but child-rearing, and are the ones who do the home maintenance (the double shift), this makes it very difficult indeed for them to progress in careers which demand long hours of work.

In fact, you have thousands of individual women making very similar decisions about their careers and their working lives which are founded on both economics and on lifestyle issues. Thanks to the law reform instigated after pressure from feminists, there is now maternity leave. What this means is that if you are in a permanent job (as opposed to a casual or contract job) and you are pregnant, you might have a number of months' leave. In most jobs this involves a year's leave without pay, but some offer three months with pay as well. Obviously, having no pay is not easy and this means that having children is very costly indeed. Nevertheless, it is done. But often after the birth, when the child is a few months old, decisions have to be made about work and about care for the child. There are a number of factors which mitigate against women returning to their old jobs.

Firstly, there is a good deal of social pressure for women to stay at home with their children. This might seem old-fashioned, and it probably is, but people tend to believe (with the most flimsy of evidence, or none at all!) that children are better off at home. Mothers who go back to work often feel enormously guilty about it because of this. Also, it can be very difficult indeed to find decent childcare which is affordable and which is of good quality. Childcare is very expensive indeed. When women earn little, using childcare at all can be financially unfeasible. Unless, of course, you can manage to persuade your mother or another relative to come on board!!

Secondly, for these reasons women often prefer to work part-time, which seems like a compromise. If they can't do this at their former workplace, they go to one where they can work more flexible hours. Often, also they choose a workplace close to home which cuts down travelling time and therefore childcare complications. It is in this scenario that women are prey to casual and contract jobs. Effectively they move from permanent jobs with the benefits of sick leave, annual leave, maternity leave and so on to casual or contract employment with none of these things.

Thirdly, if they have a partner, you might well ask why it is that the woman's career undergoes these changes through having children whereas the man's does not. Despite the common belief that there are more 'househusbands' than before, they are very rare indeed, accounting for about 3 per cent of people at home with children. Why don't men stay at home and look after their children? There are probably two reasons for this. The first is that because men tend to earn more than women, the decision is purely an economic one—it is cheaper for the woman to do it. The second reason, which is more profound, is that staying at home is a gendered occupation. It is seen as 'women's work'. Men feel unmasculine taking children to kinder-garten, working in the school canteen, doing volunteer work in the toy library. Indeed, some research shows that men in these situations are either positively alienated by the other parents (who are women) or they are praised and congratulated to an embarrassing extent about their role. But it comes down to the issues of gender socialisation (how we are raised) in the end—work is the place for men and home is the place for women. Don't you think?

So, by and large, it is women's domestic roles which seem to work against them achieving highly in their careers. For women who don't have children, then, it is possible that they are in a better position. Indeed, it might well be that this is recognised by those who choose not to have children and by those who have their children in their late thirties or early forties when they have consolidated their careers, are better off financially and are therefore better equipped to break their careers without suffering the costs which younger women do.

Equal employment opportunities

The reason why childless women are better off in the workforce than those with children (as a general rule) is partly because of equal employment opportunities. As I said earlier, until EEO it was perfectly legal and possible to reject women for jobs or promotion because they were women. No problem. It was often argued that young women would inevitably have children, so hiring them and training them was a waste of time. This is an example of that all-pervasive idea that the community bears no responsibility for children, that childbearing and childrearing are a private matter which should not encroach on the workplace at all. Hopefully, this notion is starting to change a little with some workplaces making noises about 'family friendliness'. On top of having maternity leave, this means a little flexibility when children are ill so that parents do not have to take sick leave to care for them, but can use something called 'family leave'. Similarly, some workplaces now have paternity leave for men whose partners are having babies. It is taken at the time of the birth or adoption and can last for two weeks.

But, apart from these changes in the culture of the workplace (and please remember these changes are the exception rather than the rule), it is now possible to get some redress if you believe your sex has led to discrimination against you in the workplace. This can mean anything from not getting the job or promotion, to having to wear silly clothes or make-up which sexualise you, or having a gendered culture in the workplace which makes you feel less than comfortable.

If you think that any of these things apply to you, in most countries you can now lodge a complaint. For example, in Australia there is an Equal Opportunity Tribunal whose job it is to sort out complaints of discrimination on a number of grounds. Yes, it is complaint-based which probably means that a lot of cases go by. This is because it can be an expensive and frightening thing to take your employer to the tribunal. You need a lot of courage to do it.

When the tribunal has heard your case, and the case of your employer, it makes a decision. If the tribunal rules in your favour, this can involve things such as getting the job or promotion (although working relationships can be tricky!), or being compensated for earnings you have lost, or a ruling can even be made which says you don't have to wear a particular colour of lipstick.

This tribunal is a bit like a watchdog. Its job is to resolve complaints (a bit like a court does). It listens to both sides of the argument and the bottom line is that employers must not act in a way which discriminates against women—either formally or informally. The other thing it deals with is cases of sexual harassment.

Sexual harassment

This deserves its own section because it is something much discussed and often misunderstood!

Sexual harassment is understood to be primarily something men do to women. This might be because men are usually senior to women in the workplace. There have been a few reported cases of women doing it to men (again when they are senior to them) but they are very rare indeed. What sexual harassment consists of is behaviour or speech which is bullying. But it is different from ordinary bullying to get what you want, because it is sexual.

It can consist of such things as making sexual remarks about co-workers, their bodies or clothes or what they might do in bed. It can involve staring at women's breasts. It can mean some physical activity—brushing past, touching inappropriate parts of the body (that's putting it nicely!), or even trying to make the victim touch the perpetrator. It might involve pressuring a woman to go out on a date. It often involves pornography being pinned up in canteens or other places where women have to look at it.

I'm not suggesting for a moment that females are such pathetic creatures that they cannot handle these things. Who hasn't? But two points about sexual harassment must be made. Firstly, because the pattern is that men do it women on the whole, and usually it is men who have power over the women, resisting the harassment can mean more than refusing to go out on a date. It can mean your job and your livelihood.

Secondly, a distinction must be made between sexual behaviour and sexual harassment. No one minds people meeting at work and having relationships. What is wrong with that?! It is very common. But sexual harassment is completely different. Sexual harassment is ugly. Sexual harassment is nasty. It can go on for a long time. It is both personal and impersonal. It is personal for the women involved who feel threatened and often just leave. It is impersonal because it is often about simply making the workplace comfortable for men and uncomfortable for women.

You might have heard people complain that sexual harassment legislation is an example of 'feminazis' trying to control and patrol people's relationships. That it is an attempt to desexualise workplaces and relationships. That men are trying to be complimentary or seductive. Well, such comments say more about the people who make them than about anything else, because it shows that they can't distinguish between bullying and mutual sexual attraction.

Yet it can be a difficult issue because human communication is complicated and sexual harassment can be both forceful and subtle. But its purpose isn't complicated. Its purpose is both to threaten women and make them feel uncomfortable and to possibly facilitate some sexual contact from someone who is unwilling to have it. Yuk.

If it happens to you, or to someone you know, you should nip it in bud if you can. This can be done in the first place by using words which will permanently put him off. If it continues beyond this, it might be as well to contact someone in your union who can give you advice (that is one of the reasons they are there!). Also, you can talk to one of the people in your place of work or your educational institution who are trained in these matters (sometimes called Equity Advisers)—if you are lucky enough to have them!! They will be able to give you your options and possibly take action on your behalf to sort it out. Which is marvellous. Failing all this you can approach the Equal Employment Commission who will be able to tell you what they can do for you.

But don't ever think you have to put up with it. Don't let your friends put up with it either. If you put up with it nothing will change. If you make a stand, and you give support to others making a stand, it is just possible that we will be able to change the culture of the workplace so that sexual harassment is completely and utterly unheard of. Wouldn't that be nice?

I walked down a beach with a friend once and we were talking about what we would say to our daughters if we could give them just one piece of advice. She said 'Choose the right man', I said 'Make sure you can always earn a good living so men don't matter to you economically'. What do you think?

glossary

Abortion

The termination of a pregnancy either through a surgical procedure or through the use of drugs.

Abortifacients

Drugs used to induce abortion.

Acupuncture

A Chinese medical technique where small needles, which are thought to simulate energy currents, are inserted into parts of the body. It has been practised for thousands of years in China and is used for a wide variety of complaints.

Androgyny

A personality type where the best bits of masculinity and femininity are combined.

Anorexia nervosa

An eating disorder characterised by a distorted body image, refusal of food, and excess exercise in order to induce weight loss.

Baby boomers

Name given to the generation born soon after the Second World War (between the years 1945 and 1961).

Bach flower remedies

Bach flower remedies were developed by Edward Bach in the 1930s in England. Using flower extracts, they are used to treat mood states and personal traits—in other words, emotional rather than physical problems.

Beauty pageants

Largely extinct competitions for women based on an evaluation of their bodies.

Beauty myth

Naomi Wolf's term for the pressure on women to conform to a prescribed image of female beauty.

Bisexuality

A sexual identity where the individual has sexual relationships with, or is sexually attracted to, people of both sexes.

Bulimia nervosa

An eating disorder characterised by overeating and induced vomiting.

Contraception

A variety of techniques by which conception is avoided. These include condoms, diaphragms, interuterine devices (IUDs), the contraceptive pill, tubal ligation and vasectomy.

Capitalism

An economic system in which property (such as the means of production, distribution and exchange) is held by private owners instead of being owned by the state. Capitalist countries are democratic, on the whole, and favour less (rather than more) government intervention in people's lives.

Cosmetic industry

The industry which produces products thought to improve people's looks such as hair removal creams and waxes, hair dyes, hair shampoos and conditioners, hair gel, hair spray, hair curling products, moisturisers, cleansers, toners, face masks, blackhead removers, facial scrubs, foundation, nail polish, nail polish remover, bath oils, bath salts, bubble bath, soap, lipstick, blusher, mascara, eye liner, eye gel, eye whitener, false eyelashes, false nails, and lip liner. It also includes such services as massage, manicures, pedicures, eyelash tinting, eyebrow tinting, electrolysis, body wraps and chemical skin peels.

Cosmetic surgery

Medical procedures dedicated to improve people's looks. These can include breast enlargements, breast reductions, face lifts, collagen injections into the lips, tummy tucks, removal of the lower ribs, liposuction, muscle implants, rhinoplasty (nose jobs), eye widening and eye reduction, and skin tinting.

Cultural feminism

A strand of feminism linked to radical feminism which believes that women and men are very different. Women are thought to have a number of characteristics such as nurturance, co-operation, non-violence and care for others which have been devalued in patriarchal culture and which should be reclaimed by women as being far more life-enhancing than the characteristics of patriarchy.

Denfeld, Rene

Young American author of *The New Victorians. A Young Woman's Challenge to the Old Feminist Order* which was published in 1995 by Allen & Unwin. A member of what has come to be known as the 'third wave' of feminism.

Diet industry

The industry which sells low-calorie food, dieting programs, exercise programs, exercise videos, various drugs which are thought to improve weight loss, dieting books and low-calorie food delivery services.

Domestic violence

The term for violence which occurs between members of a family, usually within the family home. It is also criminal assault.

Direct action

A kind of demonstration where protesters attempt to stop something occurring (for example the transportation of nuclear fuel or the holding of a beauty pageant) through disruption of the proceedings. Usually this is done using peaceful obstruction.

Discrimination

Discrimination occurs when a person is denied access to goods and services, or is treated differently from someone else because of their sex, race, ethnicity, sexual orientation, religious beliefs, physical ability or age.

Eating disorders

A collection of disorders which focus on the relationship between food intake and perceived body shape. They are characterised by the following: reduction of food intake, excess exercise, compulsive eating, purging (using laxatives), and vomiting. They affect many more women than men.

Eco-feminism

A stream of feminist theory which makes a connection between patriarchal society and environmental destruction.

Egalitarian

A term used to describe relations between people or groups of people which are equal in terms of power.

Epidural

An anaesthetic commonly used in birth which is injected into the base of the spine and which numbs the lower half of the body.

Episiotomy

A technique used in birth during the delivery. An incision is made in the perineum (between the anus and the vulva).

Equal opportunities

A collection of acts of law which make it illegal for individuals or organisations to discriminate against people on the grounds of their sex, race, ethnicity, sexual orientation, physical ability or age.

Equal pay

A term for the equal payment to men and women for undertaking the same work.

Face lift

A surgical procedure where the skin of the face is partially removed or pinned behind the ears. It is thought to make the recipient look younger.

Fashion industry

The industry which controls what is, and what is not, deemed 'fashionable'. It involves the design centres, magazines and clothing styles which change regularly in order that people buy new clothes.

The Feminine Mystique

A landmark book by Betty Friedan published in the USA in 1963. It brought to light some of the limitations women were experiencing at this time.

Femininity

Femininity is a model for female perfection. Although it changes over time, some of its enduring features are passivity, empathy, slimness and heterosexuality.

Feminism

An umbrella term for a broad range of theory which attempts to explain why men and women are treated so differently in societies. It also includes ideas about how to make societies more equal.

French feminism

Helene Cixous, Julia Kristeva and Luce Irigaray are among the most influential writers from this school of feminist writing. They are interested in the ways in which language and writing helps to determine the ways we think and the way we act.

Freud, Sigmund

An Austrian physician who, in the early part of the twentieth century, founded the discipline of psychoanalysis. He was particularly interested in the unconscious and in sexuality.

Game girls

Game girls design and develop computer games which challenge some of the norms. They have females as the main protagonists who take on patriarchal figures such as 'big daddy mainframe' computers.

Geekgirls

Geekgirls run a 'zine on the internet and have a web site. They are interested in gender relations in cyberspace and are keen to ensure not only that women use the internet for their own purposes, but that they develop its shape and ethos. You can find them at *http:\\www.geekgirl.com.au*

Gender

A term used to denote the characteristics which societies view as desirable for a particular sex. Gender is thought to be socially constructed rather than natural, being a result of gender socialisation.

Genetics

A field of biological science which investigates the relationship between our genes (which we inherit from our parents) and our physical and mental development.

Glass ceiling

Commonly used to mean the barrier which prevents women from reaching the top in various professions.

Grassroots movement

This is used to describe a technique for social reform which is aimed at change at a community level rather than using formal institutions and attempting change from the top down.

Hand lifts

A cosmetic surgery procedure which is aimed at making hands look younger by decreasing the size of veins and tightening the skin.

Heterosexuality

A form of sexuality involving men and women. It is the dominant form of sexuality in patriarchies and, some argue, is forced upon us.

Homoeopathy

Homoeopathy is based on the principle of treating 'like with like'. Using essences and plant extracts, homoeopaths use the essence or extract which is aligned with the physical problem being suffered by the patient. In doing so, the body's natural defences are increased in order to fight the illness.

Homosexuality

A sexual identity where the individual has sexual relationships with, or is sexually attracted to people of the same sex.

Hormone Replacement Therapy

A medical treatment for menopausal women which replaces the hormones which are inactive after menopause. It is thought to relieve the symptoms of menopause and protect women from heart disease and osteoporosis.

Housewife

A role where women stay at home and out of the paid workforce in order to look after her family. Fewer and fewer women are now undertaking this role which is probably one of the most undervalued in society.

'Hysterical woman'

A term arising from the Greek word for uterus, used to label women as somehow prone, because of possessing a uterus, to being emotional.

Ideology

Ideology was used by Karl Marx and later developed by the Italian Marxist Antonio Gramsci. Ideology refers to individual ideas and collections of ideas which serve the purposes of the ruling class. Extremely adaptable, these ideas involve claims of truth which can effectively persuade individuals to both believe in them and to act against their own best interests because of them.

Induction

Induction is used to artificially start labour in a pregnant woman. It is achieved using an intravenous drip of oxytocin, through the application of prostaglandin pessaries and through breaking the amniotic sack.

Invitro-fertilisation

This effectively means 'fertilisation in glass' and refers to the artificial joining together of a female ovum and male sperm to produce a zygote (embryo) which is then placed in the woman's uterus in the hope that it will implant.

Liberal feminism

An early strand of feminism which is dedicated to transforming the institutions of society in order that women are better represented within them. It has been criticised for being very individualistic (seeking to improve the wellbeing of individuals rather than women as a group) and middle class (because its activities are aimed at women who are professionals rather than working class women).

Liposuction

A cosmetic surgery technique which is aimed at removing body fat through, simply, vacuuming out fat cells. It leads to extensive bruising and, unless it is done efficiently, a rather bumpy appearance.

Marxist feminism

A strand of feminism which is based on Marxism. As such, its central belief is that the source of female oppression is capitalism, and class relations. Consequently, the end to such subordination is envisaged with the demise of capitalism and class society.

Masculinity

Like femininity, masculinity is seen as a gendered conception of perfection—this time for males. Its qualities are different for different societies and at different points in history. Some of the qualities seen as masculine in contemporary Western societies are physical strength, individualism, heterosexuality, competitiveness, rationality and being unemotional.

Media

Describes a method of transmitting information. 'The media' is usually used in place of the 'mass' media—where one source of information and opinion is transmitted to many (i.e. television, newspapers, radio, the internet).

Menopause

This is the time in a woman's life where she moves from a potentially fertile state of ovulation and menstruation, to a post-fertile state where her production of oestrogen falls away.

Nature

This is often used as an adjective to mean a state of being which is removed from the influences of society. Of course, it also refers to our environment. When used in terms of gender, it is often meant to convey a message of purity so that gender relations are seen as somehow genetically determined rather than socially determined in order that these gender relations are seen as immutable.

Obesity

A medically defined condition where the individual weighs 20 per cent or more over their ideal weight.

'Obstructed menses'

A now obsolete term which was a synonym for pregnancy. Various 'cures' for this condition were sold which were, in fact, abortifacients.

Patriarchy

A social system in which all men have power over all women. This power is manifest both in public office where men control all the great avenues of power, and in private relationships where men are thought to both control and dominate women.

Pornography

Both written and visual material which depict explicit sexual acts. These acts carry with them an inherent power imbalance (in heterosexual pornography) where the female is constructed as both dominated by the male, and as a sex object.

Postmodern feminism

A strand of feminism which is not reliant on 'meta-theory' which attempts to theorise using large explanatory tools. Instead, postmodern feminism is interested in smaller theoretical tools which attempt to deal with localised problems and utilise a number of intersecting structures such as race, sex, class, disability and sexuality. It has been criticised by some feminists for being apolitical and resisting a strong gender analysis.

Pre-menstrual syndrome

A medically-defined 'syndrome' which is ill-defined but describes a range of symptoms which can be associated (for some women) with menstruation, such as fluid retention, mood swings and weight gain.

'Private' sphere

A term used to designate the world outside the paid workforce. Usually, it is taken to mean the home and the domestic duties undertaken within it, usually by women. In addition it is sometimes used to describe paid employment which is not unlike domestic duties such as nursing, childcare, teaching, work in the hospitality industry—again, work dominated by women.

Professional Beauty Qualification (PBQ)

Coined by Naomi Wolf in *The Beauty Myth*, this refers to the increasing requirement that women employed in particular fields conform to a specific 'look'. She also argues that more and more careers are being dominated by the PBQ.

Psychoanalytic feminism

A collection of feminist theories which are not based on a material analysis (ones which emphasise economics) but emphasise the unconscious processes which help to sustain patriarchy. These theories are sometimes based on Freud, but also on more recent writers such as Jacques Lacan.

'Public' sphere

This is taken to mean the areas of paid work which take place outside the home, and involve activities unlike those undertaken at home. Most professional careers dominated by men are within the public sphere, and they have a large impact on public institutions and consequently, on private lives.

Radical feminism

A strand of feminism which uses the central idea that most societies are patriarchies. Radical feminism tends to place an emphasis on bodies, sexuality and reproduction in its analysis of patriarchal power and its maintenance.

Reproduction

This term has two meanings. Firstly, it is used to designate the process of fertilisation, pregnancy and birth. Secondly, it refers to the household duties which are necessary to ensure that people are equipped to enter the workforce. Because of this, Marxist feminists in particular argue that reproduction is the foundation of the economy since without it, workers would be unable to function.

Riot grrrls

A new term used to describe the women involved in a style of rock music which is, in essence, feminist. Much of this music is played in pubs and clubs rather than being produced by large record companies.

Roiphe, Katie

Author of *The Morning After. Sex, Fear and Feminism* which is a critique of second wave feminism and, in particular, of sexual harassment legislation which she believes is draconian.

Sadomasochism

A sexual practice also known by the abbreviation 'S and M' which involves the use of power and physical pain. Many of its proponents argue that sadomasochism simply plays out many of the power issues which are involved in sexual practices generally.

Sex

In feminist literature, sex is taken to mean the biological categories of male and female. As such, it is differentiated from 'gender' which is socially constructed.

Sexuality

Although sometimes seen as inherently linked to reproduction (and, therefore, heterosexuality), sexuality refers to the wide variety of sexual practices and identities which people engage in.

'Sexual double standard'

An increasingly obsolete term which refers to the standards applied to female and male sexual behaviour. Promiscuity in males is thought to carry with it social cachet, but for females it brings with it social disapproval. Consequently, although there are many derogatory names for females thought to be very active sexually, while there are none for men.

Sexual harassment

A range of bullying behaviours predominantly aimed at women which are based on sexuality and power.

Sexual orientation

Used to describe whether a person considers themselves heterosexual (interested in having sexual partners from the opposite sex), homosexual (interested in partners of the same sex), or bisexual (interested in partners of both sexes).

Sex worker

Somebody who works in the sex industry. Usually someone who engages in sexual activity for money.

Sisterhood

A term used to designate women as a group and, in particular, those who are feminists and who work for gender equity.

Socialisation

A life-long process which begins in childhood where the individual is inducted into the mores and behaviour thought to be appropriate socially.

Socialist feminism

A strand of feminism which is based on the theory of patriarchy and on a material analysis. Socialist feminists believe that these two structures are inextricably bound together and produce the gender relations particular to any society.

Spicegirls

A group of five young British women whose trademark is 'girl power' and who have enjoyed huge popularity among ten to fourteen year old girls in the late 1990s.

Surrogacy

A method of reproduction for infertile couples who hire a woman to carry their child to term. Biologically the baby can be the couples', or partly the surrogate mother's, or not be biologically connected to any of them, using a donor's egg and sperm.

Swingers

A term used for people who swap sexual partners at parties. It has also been called 'wife-swapping', but 'swingers' implies a more proactive role for the women.

Transsexuals

Also known as 'transgendered', transsexuals are people who have undergone surgery and hormone treatment to change their sex.

Transvestites

Transvestites are usually men who enjoy wearing women's clothing.

Tummy tucks

A vernacular term for a cosmetic surgery procedure where a person's midriff is reduced in size.

Wise women

Wise women were the women in the pre-scientific era whose responsibility it was to maintain the community's health. They were wiped out during the witch hunts in Western Europe.

Wolf, Naomi

American author of *The Beauty Myth*, *Fire with Fire* and *Promiscuities*. She is sometimes referred to as a 'third wave' feminist.

further
reading

There are many books about the issues we have looked at. Here is a list of some of the best.

Feminism

Bell, Diane & Klein, Renate (eds), 1996, *Radically Speaking. Feminism Reclaimed,* Spinifex Press.

Bulbeck, Chilla 1997, *Living Feminism. The Impact of the Women's Movement on Three Generations of Australian Women,* Cambridge University Press.

Evans, Mary 1995, *The Woman Question,* Sage Publications.

Greer, Germaine 1971, *The Female Eunuch,* Paladin.

Tong, Rosemarie 1993, *Feminist Thought. A Comprehensive Introduction,* Unwin Hyman.

Wolf, Naomi 1993, *Fire With Fire. The New Female Power and How it Will Change the Twenty First Century,* Chatto and Windus.

Bodies

Cooke, Kaz 1994, *Real Gorgeous. The Truth About Body and Beauty,* Allen & Unwin.

Corrigan, Annette & Meredyth, Denise 1997, 'The body politic' in *Contemporary Australian Feminism 2,* ed. Kate Pritchard Hughes, Addison Wesley Longman.

Davis, Kathy 1995, *Reshaping the Female Body: The Dilemma of Cosmetic Surgery,* Routledge.

Johnston, Joni E. 1994, *Appearance Obsession. Learning to Love the Way You Look,* Health Communications Inc.

Landey, Nicole (ed.), 1994, *Many Mirrors: Body Image and Social Relations,* Rutgers University Press.

Wolf, Naomi 1991, *The Beauty Myth. How Images of Beauty are Used Against Women,* Vintage.

Relationships

Debold, Elizabeth, Wilson, Marie & Malave, Idelisse 1994, *Mother Daughter Revolution. From Good Girls to Great Women,* Doubleday.

Gray, John 1993, *Men are From Mars and Women are From Venus,* Thorsens.

Miedzian, Miriam 1991, *Boys Will be Boys. Breaking the Link Between Masculinity and Violence.* Women's Press.

Morton, Tom 1997, *Altered Mates. The Man Question,* Allen & Unwin.

Raymond, Janice G. 1986, *A Passion For Friends. Towards a Philosophy of Female Affection,* Women's Press.

Sexuality

Bram, Dijkstra 1996, *Evil Sisters: The Threat of Women's Sexuality and the Cult of Manhood,* Alfred Knopf.

Jackson, Stevi, & Scott, Sue (eds), 1996, *Feminism and Sexuality: A Reader,* Columbia University Press.

Jeffreys, Sheila 1990, *AntiClimax. A Feminist Perspective on the Sexual Revolution,* Women's Press.

Segal, Lynne 1994, *Straight Sex. The Politics of Pleasure,* Women's Press.

Weeks, Jeffrey 1991, *Against Nature: Essays on History, Sexuality and Identity,* Rivers Oram Press.

Health

Ammer, Christine 1995, *The New A to Z of Women's Health: A Concise Encyclopedia,* Facts on File.

Boston Women's Health Collective, 1985, *The New Our Bodies Ourselves,* Penguin.

Broom, Dorothy H. 1991, *Damned if We Do: Contradictions in Women's Health Care,* Allen & Unwin.

Doyal, Lesley 1995, *What Makes Women Sick: Gender and the Political Economy of Health,* Macmillan.

Ehrenreich, Barbara & English, Deidre 1979, *For Her Own Good: 150 Years of the Experts' Advice to Women,* Pluto Press.

Saltman, Deborah 1997, 'Feminism and the health care movement' in *Contemporary Australian Feminism 2*, ed. Kate Pritchard Hughes, Addison Wesley Longman.

Work

Adkins, Lisa 1994, *Gendered Work: Sexuality, Family and the Labour Market,* Oxford University Press.

Itzin Catherine & Newman, Janet 1995, *Gender, Culture and Organisational Change: Putting Theory into Practice,* Routledge.

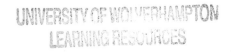

Lehrman, Karen 1997, *The Lipstick Proviso: Women, Sex and Power in the Real World*, Doubleday.

MacEwen Scott, Alison (ed.) 1994, *Gender Segregation and Social Change: Men and Women in Changing Labour Markets,* Oxford University Press.

Probert, Belinda & Wilson, Bruce W. 1993, *Pink Collar Blues: Work, Gender and Technology*, Melbourne University Press.

Wise, Sue & Stanley, Liz 1987, *Georgie Porgie. Sexual Harassment in Everyday Life*, Pandora.